THE TWO CITIES OF GOD

The Two Cities of God

The Church's Responsibility for the Earthly City

Edited by

Carl E. Braaten and Robert W. Jenson

WILLIAM B. EERDMANS PUBLISHING COMPANY
GRAND RAPIDS, MICHIGAN / CAMBRIDGE, U.K.

© 1997 Wm. B. Eerdmans Publishing Co.
255 Jefferson Ave. S.E., Grand Rapids, Michigan 49503 /
P.O. Box 163, Cambridge CB3 9PU U.K.

Printed in the United States of America

02 01 00 99 98 97   7 6 5 4 3 2 1

Library of Congress Cataloging-in-Publication Data

The two cities of God: the church's responsibility for the earthly city /
edited by Carl E. Braaten and Robert W. Jenson.
p.   cm.
Papers presented at conferences held Oct. 8-9, 1995,
at St. John's Lutheran Church, Northfield, Minn.; Oct. 15-16, 1995,
at Grace Lutheran Church, Lancaster, Pa.;
and at Immanuel Lutheran Church, New York, N.Y.
Includes bibliographical references.
ISBN 0-8028-4304-2 (alk. paper)
1. Church and the world — Congresses.
I. Braaten, Carl E., 1929-   . II. Jenson, Robert W.
BR115.W6T86   1997
261'.1 — dc21   97-8589
CIP

Contents

Preface   vii
   Carl E. Braaten and Robert W. Jenson

The Church's Responsibility for the World   1
   Robert W. Jenson

The Two Cities in Christian Scripture   11
   Christopher R. Seitz

Augustine's City of God Today   28
   Robert L. Wilken

Natural Law in Theology and Ethics   42
   Carl E. Braaten

The Church's Political Hopes for the World;
or, Diognetus Revisited   59
   George Weigel

Whose Crisis of Faith? Culture, Faith,
and the American Academy   78
   Anthony Ugolnik

The Calling of the Church in Economic Life   95
   Robert Benne

The Venture of Marriage   117
   Gilbert Meilaender

Contributors   133

Preface

The chapters of this book offer perspectives on a "theology of the world." They were presented as papers at two conferences sponsored by the Center for Catholic and Evangelical Theology. "The Left Hand of God" was the theme of the first conference, held at St. John's Lutheran Church, Northfield, Minnesota, October 8-9, and at Grace Lutheran Church, Lancaster, Pennyslvania, October 15-16, 1995. "Orthopraxy for the Secular City" was the theme of the second conference, held at Immanuel Lutheran Church, New York City, January 22, 1996. The chapter on natural law in Protestant theology by Carl E. Braaten was presented as a paper at a conference sponsored by the Ethics and Public Policy Center, Washington, D.C., in 1991.

The "Left Hand of God" was Martin Luther's image of the way God administers the daily affairs of human existence: marriage and family, political, economic, and cultural life. With his "right hand" God rules by the gospel and commissions the church to preach the good news of salvation to all the world. The problem of the relation between the "two hands" has been one of the thorniest in theology. The tendency among conservatives has been to separate them, whereas liberals have tended to identify them.

Old questions continue to be debated in church and theology. What does Jerusalem have to do with Athens? What does Christ have to do with culture? What does the church have to do with the world? What does faith have to do with works, creeds with deeds? Our conferences rephrased the question in this way: How does/should the church relate to the secular world? The standard dogma of the 1960s was: Let the world set the agenda! Such a perspective has often caused the American church merely to reflect, rather than inform and lead, the society in which it lives. Surely it must be the other way around!

Christians claim that the church is the one community given knowledge of God's will for the world. However arrogant this sounds, the church that is no longer willing to sustain such a claim has arguably lost its reason for existence. The first task of the church, precisely in the modern secular city, is to be true to her own self as the Body of Christ in the world. By being nothing less than the community of God's love, the church confronts the city with the truth of the city's own nature and destiny. The church serves the city best by giving it the means to see itself truthfully.

The title of this book is *The Two Cities of God*, which, of course, refers to the biblical images of the earthly city and the heavenly city. The biblical account of salvation starts with the story of Adam and Eve in the Garden of Eden and ends with a vision of the saints in the heavenly city of Jerusalem. The intervening history of salvation is intertwined with the city. The road from paradise lost to paradise regained runs through the great cities built by the children of Cain — Babel, Babylon, Sodom, Nineveh. Finally, the earthly Jerusalem became the battleground on which Christ defeated the "powers and principalities."

We believe that the church's faithful service in the world and its cities must begin and end with her life in the communion of the triune God. As such she is a sign and agent of the heavenly city within and for the earthly city. The rites and liturgies of the new community are her most urgent witness, since in them the church's true identity appears. Thus the church's task of renewal and reform in the city is the renewal of her own local eucharistic communities. Stanley Hauerwas has put it pointedly: "The church does not *have* a social ethic; the church *is* a social ethic."

CARL E. BRAATEN
ROBERT W. JENSON

The Church's Responsibility for the World

ROBERT W. JENSON

I

The question about the church's responsibility for the world has been much discussed, and particularly since the world of Christendom ceased to constitute itself the secular world. Usually the question is discussed in terms of "shoulds" or "oughts": "What responsibility does the church have for the world?" is taken to be equivalent with "What ought the church do about or for the world?" The question must of course be discussed in this form, and this was indeed the initiating concern of the conference for which this essay was written. I will eventually come to it.

But only a little acquaintance with recent discussion of the question must impress one with a certain lack of discipline in this discussion: almost every conceivable answer has been proposed by someone, and almost always with apparent good theological reason: "The church ought to get in on the world's action." "The church ought to provide an entire alternative to the world." "The church ought to reform the world." And so on.

I want to suggest that at least part of the reason for the seemingly uncontrollable way in which we answer the question "What ought the church to do about the world?" is failure to observe or take seriously another and in my judgment prior way in which the question of the church's responsibility for the world can be construed. Let me display that other construal of the question by bluntly stating my answer to it: the church is responsible for the world in the elementary sense that were it not for the church there would be no world.

1

Nor do I mean this proposition in any subtle fashion. The church is *to blame* for the existence of all that we call the world. In stuffier terms, the church is not just morally responsible for the world but is ontologically responsible for it; and indeed is the first only because the world is the second.

Why, after all, did God create the world? According to Genesis, creation is purposeful: at each step, God determines that what is created is good, and in Hebrew as in English, "good" means "good *for*" something. Jews and Christians believe that God has something in mind for creation that is not simply the creation as it stands.

Moreover, Jews and Christians not only believe this but also claim to know *what* God's purpose was and is — namely, the coming-into-being of a particular community of creatures. So the Judaism of Christ's time taught: "it was for us that thou didst create the world" (2 Esdras 6:55). The church took over this claim, along with the rest of Judaism's doctrine of creation, and applied it to herself: "for the church's sake the cosmos was framed" (Hermas, *Vision* II.4.1). Even the deutero-Pauline doctrine that "All things were created through . . . and for" Christ depends on the doctrine that all things were created for the church, for Christ appears in that passage of Colossians precisely as "he is the head of . . . the church" (1:15-20).

The world, in other words, is there as the presupposition of the church; the world is there as what God must have in order to have a church. Or as Karl Barth put it — although in good Protestant fashion avoiding the notion of church — the world is the "outer basis" of "the covenant."

And it is the *actual* covenant that is the purpose of creation, the covenant that establishes a *community of redeemed sinful creatures*. Remaining with the Colossians passage, the very reason that Christ is the one for whom and through whom all is created is that he makes "peace through the blood of his cross."

II

We are now in a position to say why God created the world, and we will do so in a series of steps. First, if there is to be a community of redeemed sinful creatures, there must be creatures, and therefore there is the creation. Already this basic point excludes nearly all recently fashionable proposals about the ethical responsibility of the church for the world. But we can go on.

Second, if there is to be a community of redeemed sinful creatures, there must be communal creatures. The marks that differentiate human creatures from others are often sought in supposed unique endowments of the *species* — that is to say, in endowments that each of us has as an individual. But it is not taught that I am the goal of creation, or that any number of such I's together are the goal of creation. It is the community of the church that is the goal of creation.

The peculiarity of the human creature is its call into community: it belongs to the story of our creation that the Creator addresses us in expectation of response, and just so brings us into community with him. Moreover, as the story of Genesis runs, it is just so that he also sets us in families with each other, families that are not strictly biological phenomena but require to be protected by law and custom and religious blessing, and so are communities in the full sense.

Third, if there is to be a community of redeemed sinful creatures, the immediately involved creatures must be sinners. *Therefore,* in the insight of the most radical Christian thinkers, God allows sin; and his allowing of sin cannot be fully separated from his allowing of creatures. As Luther said in the Large Catechism, "God created us just in order to redeem us" ("Denn er hat uns eben dazu geschaffen dass er uns erlösete"; *Bekenntnisschriften . . . ,* 660.33-34.) The Hegelian or Tillichian ideas that creation and fall are more or less the same thing cannot stand. But neither can the usual unthinking idea that redemption is a rescue operation after intruding disaster.

And we must surely consider this particular determination of God's purpose also the other way around, to see what it says about the church herself. It is not an ideal church, or an invisible church, or a number of saints who meet only in the mind of God that is the goal of creation. It is the actual church, the church whose servants we are, the sometimes lamentably institutionalized and sometimes lamentably privatized church, the *corpus mixtum* of those who belong in it and those who do not, the church Luther called "a big sinner" (feminine, *eine grosse Sünderin*) that is the reason of creation, the community for the sake of which God needs a creation.

Fourth and finally in this series, if there is to be a community of redeemed sinful creatures, there must be redeemable creatures — that is, creatures whose destiny is not exhausted in the initial terms of their creatureliness, and thus creatures for whom death is not necessarily the end of the story. In order for there to be the redeemed community, there must be we creatures who can live neither with death nor without it, who must always try to come to terms with death and can never succeed.

Here, too, there is a converse we should note. The church that is the goal of creation can herself be neither limited by death nor yet, short of the last day, free of it. The church is essentially on both sides of the line of death: she is the pilgrim church on earth that nevertheless has more members on the other side of death than on this side of it. The church that is creation's goal is intrinsically the church of striving *and* perfected saints. If we are to understand the way in which the church is the purpose of creation, and so the church's ethical responsibility for the world, we cannot abstract from the membership of Stephen and Sergius and of my father-in-law John Rockne and of all the other human members of the heavenly host.

III

And now it is indeed time to move on to the ethical form of our question: What ought the church to do about the world? I will begin with negations, to clear the ground, for the ontological dependence of the world on the church immediately excludes some popular, or recently popular, positions.

A first excluded position is this: the slogan that has dominated the mainline churches' social and evangelistic activity for fifty years — that the world must set the church's agenda — is precisely and comprehensively false. It would not even be correct to turn it around and say that the church should set the agenda for the world, not because the proposition is too strong but because even this proposition is not yet strong enough. The true statement is that the church *is* the world's agenda. What the world is there to do is to provide the raw materials out of which God creates his church.

Such a claim is, of course, unlikely to be widely believed, in the churches as well as in the world. But it is in fact an intrinsically highly plausible proposition. Its negative side is even empirically obvious: that the world on its own, apart from the church, *has* no agenda.

The very notion of an "agenda" for the world, of a goal of worldly existence and of a historical path to it, is unknown in the world apart from the intrusion of the biblical faiths. Only where the descendants of Abraham have propagandized is the world aware that it might have a reason for being, a purpose beyond itself. Indeed, the great religions are devoted precisely, from the viewpoint of Abrahamic faith, to cultivating the *absence* of any universal or cosmic agenda.

In the Western world, however, the notion of a universal agenda has come to seem natural because of the Western world's peculiar relation to biblical faith. The church created the civilization of Europe and its descendent cultures, and so the idea of an agenda for the world's history did become part of Western civilization.

That the West has now cut its connection to the church and the church's gospel results in something more drastic than the normal mere absence of agenda. We now have long experience of what that something more is: it is not mere disorder; it is vindictive disorder, chaos. Alexander Solzhenitsyn has suggested that all the warfare since the outbreak of the First World War has in fact been one long civil war of Western civilization, a civil war occasioned precisely by the repeated appearance of nihilistic movements, from the sheer mindless nationalism of many parties to the first war, to Hitlerism and Stalinism, and now again back to the older style.

A second excluded position is closely related to the first: we have regularly been told during the last fifty years that the church should be looking around the world to see where God is at work and jump in to work with him. But this advice is impossible of fulfillment. From one point of view, God is at work in the world everywhere. But if we are to speak of God's *location*, of the place in the world *from* which he is at work in it, then the church is herself that location. The point is, after all, theologically elementary: *Christ* is God's located presence in the world; to be located he has to have a *body;* the church, says the New Testament, is that body of Christ.

IV

I can postpone no longer. What is the church's moral responsibility for the world? It is to preserve the being of the world, as the world is the presupposition of the church. Thus, to see what specifically the church must do for the world, the church need only consult her own interest:

what the world needs to remain in being is what serves the mission and sanctity of the church. Here two systematic questions arise that I can neither merely skip over nor deal with in more than peremptory fashion.

First, how can the being of the world be in doubt? Where the gospel has not yet come, the being of the world cannot be doubted; there the world simply is the world is the world is the world is. . . . But where the gospel has brought awareness that God has purpose for the world, that the world might have an agenda, there the being of the world becomes a project, something that must be worked on; and then, of course, the project can fail, the world can fail its own being, can decline toward nothingness.

Second, how can the *church* do anything about the world's being? The church can do something about the world's being because God creates the world by his Word, and because the church in the world is enabled to speak that very same Word. It became dogma in Israel: "By the Word of the LORD the heavens were made" (Ps. 33:6). And in that psalm and similar passages, "the Word of the LORD" is a *terminus technicus* for the Word in the mouth of the prophets, which "will not return empty" until it does what God says by it (Isa. 55:11). The church claims to speak that word in that she claims to be one big prophetess, to be the fulfillment of the hope for the prophetic Spirit's universal outpouring.

So, finally, a basic proposition: the church's moral responsibility for the world is to speak in such a way, by audible and visible words, as to combat the world's decline toward nothingness.

V

To combat the world's decay, the church must first combat the world's endemic betrayal of its own *community*. The world exists to be a community of such sort that the church-community can exist within it; the church's responsibility is to speak in such a way as to call the world to this sort of community.

If we then ask what sort of community the church is to be, and therefore what sort of community the world must be to provide place for the church, God has already given us the answer in what we call "the Ten Commandments."

The Decalogue is intrinsically two-sided. Addressed to the synagogue or the church, the commandments have a positive sense filled by and filling the actual life of these unique communities. Thus, for example, "You shall not commit adultery" as torah for synagogue or church means, as Martin Luther put it in the *Small Catechism,* that we "live chastely and soberly in word and deed, and that each one loves and honors his or her spouse."

Addressed to the world, however, this command can have no such affirmative sense. In that context it can only lay down boundary conditions: a society must regulate sexuality by laws and customs, and whatever these laws are, the society cannot survive their widespread violation. We may hope but cannot expect that the world's marriages will be, as the pious now like to say, "covenants of faithfulness." But we *can* tell a society like America, which is dismantling its laws of marriage and does not enforce those that remain, that it is undoing its own viability as a community.

Or again, "You shall not kill," addressed to the church, is filled with the meaning it acquires in the life of the baptismal and eucharistic community. As Luther lays it out, we are to do our "neighbor no bodily harm for any reason, but help and assist him in every bodily need." Addressed to the world, this command can hardly mean so much; usually it can mean only what it meant in the first birth of civilization, that no one is to be put to death at the decision of those who have reason to wish his or her death, but only at the decision of public authorities that he or she has so acted as to forfeit life.

So the church can say to America no more than such things as that, for example, by permitting abortion on demand the nation has relapsed to barbarism and is beyond the pale of God's covenanted mercy. The church can say no more — but of course if she could pull herself together to say *that* much she would fulfill much of her current responsibility to the world. It is the church's responsibility to address the Ten Commandments, in their minimal, boundary-setting sense, to the world, in hope that thereby the world-community can be restrained from undoing itself.

The "social statements" — or whatever they may be called — of mainline denominations regularly proceed as if discerning the church's message to the world on such things as war making or fetal experimentation or euthanasia or the provision of a social safety net were a difficult and subtle task of biblical exegesis and theological reflection. It is not, and the mainline churches' pretense that it is is only a cover for their cowardice and unbelief. The Lord has told us what our community as the church can be, and what therefore the world's community minimally must be; and there is nothing equivocal or ambiguous about what he has said.

And in addition, first and last, we can pray that God will, by our instrumentality and by other means, not permit our worldly community to collapse.

VI

The next consideration is this: the world relapses toward nothingness also as it ceases to be sinful. There is a way for the world to become innocent, which is for it to become nothing. This is not intended as a quip. Jonathan Edwards early predicted America's peculiar and great temptation, that we so easily persuade ourselves that vice is its own excuse: that if I not only do wicked things but do them constantly, I cannot be to blame, since I must have been born that way or have been shaped by overwhelming social influence or be suffering from a "disease." This is of course but our particular form of the world's constant temptation to define away the difference between sin and virtue.

And there is in fact a certain innocence to the large new American *Lumpenproletariat* for whom the laws and customs of their own society have become incomprehensible; and to the Baby Boomers from whose minds the laws of the market have driven out all other standards; and to the academic theologians who can excuse anything. Genuine villains are not often recruited from such populations.

In this connection, the church's responsibility is ideological. The world always negotiates its antinomianism by some plausible set of ideas, which in the Western world are usually perversions of ideas stolen from the church. Whenever the church can gain access to the world's forums, she is responsible to debate and debunk the ideologies by which the world obfuscates the morally obvious.

America has now lived for a long time by a sort of secularized cheap grace, and the country cannot stand much more of it; and the fact that the Christian Coalition and "right-wing" bishops are among those who say this does not make it false. It *is*, for example, obvious that we cannot equate chosen or culturally accepted single parenthood with a family structure. It *is* obvious that homosexuals cannot marry, so that homosexuality cannot be a social equivalent of heterosexuality. It *is* obvious that in a just society neither such entertainers as the one formerly known as Prince nor the Fortune 500 CEOs would be remunerated as they are, or indeed in many cases remunerated at all, whatever the sacred market will bear. A gambler who gets in over his or her head is trapped in a vice, not suffering from a disease. The racism of the Los Angeles police does not justify the acquittal of a killer. Blaming someone for abandoning his children is not the same as blaming him for being poor. America transgressed the bounds of justifiable war-making long before it used nuclear explosives. And so on.

Somebody has to say such things. To say them, one must know them. And knowing them is supposed to be one of the results of doing theology. It is the church's responsibility for the world to maintain the obvious truth in the storm of the world's ideological obfuscations. It is the church's responsibility to the world to debate theology with the world.

And in this connection, too, first and last we can pray that God, by our instrumentality and in other ways, will maintain the sinfulness of the world, will keep the angels with their flaming swords at the gates of Paradise and not let the world sneak back in. The world must be kept outside Paradise, where sinners and saints are possible.

VII

Finally, the world relapses into its own nothingness when it has no hope for a destiny that is not exhausted in the initial terms of its creatureliness. The world sinks into non-being when it comes to accept that death is the end of the creaturely story, when it comes to live peacefully with death and just so also without it.

The church's responsibility for the world is to maintain the promise of a transformed creation beyond creation's end. That is, the church's responsibility for the world in the world is to preach the gospel to the world, to proclaim that one of us is already installed as Lord of the Kingdom to come.

In this connection it is vital that the gospel invites the world into the church. In some contexts we must say that God provides the church to speak the gospel to the world, in other contexts that God provides the gospel to call persons into the church. In the present context, it is the second proposition that enables our understanding. The gospel opens to the world and beckons the world into a community that already has one branch in the world to come.

We do not expect all the world to come into the church; we are now considering precisely the responsibility of the church to the world that has not entered her community. In this respect the church is an open door through which the world can see created human community reaching beyond itself and beyond death.

The saints are always fascinating to the world, and that is as it should be. A pagan who will not believe may nevertheless be maintained in his or her humanity, in his or her place as a redeemable creature, by fascination with Francis or Hildegard or any of that multitude of creatures, in all other ways like him or her, who have lived in this world to be redeemed and have in fact entered the future beyond death.

Protestantism, of course, shoots itself in the foot here. Protestant churches' failure to display their full roster to the world, their insistence on being as small and ordinary and insignificant and this-worldly as possible, is perhaps the chief thing that enfeebles their political and economic and social import. How many divisions has the Pope? A great many more than the Red Army at its prime, and every soldier of them bulletproof.

And yet, one more time and in conclusion, first and last we can pray that the world will not lose hope, that it will continue to long for it knows not what, that death will remain at once repelling and fascinating.

The Two Cities in Christian Scripture

CHRISTOPHER R. SEITZ

There is no "doctrine" of the city in Christian Scripture, no one book dedicated to the topic, no sustained treatment about how the church should exist in the city as opposed to the country or suburbs, no chapter or subdivision of a book — even one as programmatic as Deuteronomy — devoted specifically to the city. One can find no studied contrast between the perils of city life and a more contemplative rural existence. With apologies to Jacques Ellul, the city is no more of a problem for God than the country. Both places have their challenges, their potentials; and if anything the city holds far greater prospect for manifesting the presence of God than the country. "There is a river whose streams make glad the city of God [not the country]. God is in the midst of her, she shall not be moved" (Ps. 46:4-5).

When we speak of cities today, we may have in mind poverty, the homeless, shelters and soup kitchens and drugs, the problems of isolation and loneliness; or, on the other side, ambition, power, excitement, the thrall of the possible. It's not clear how neatly this picture matches city life in antiquity, for many of these matters are the result of technology, not city dwelling per se. The thrall of the possible is now beamed down by satellite onto every roof top from Tokyo to Timbuktu, from a height that leaves that tower in ancient Babel looking like, as we say in the South, a pissant by comparison.

From the very first, biblical texts tell of the building of cities: from Cain's modest construction of the first city, Enoch, in Genesis 4; to Nimrod the Great's Babylon and Akkad in Genesis 10; to the famous city and tower of Babel in Genesis 11; up to and including the heavenly

11

city Jerusalem in the Revelation to John, on the Bible's last horizon. Zion-Jerusalem is the focus of much of the Old Testament's reflection: the city of Israel's Messiah, the place where God's glory dwells. "I have set my king on Zion, my holy hill" (Ps. 2:6). This doesn't change in the New Testament, though a transformation takes place. This will make inevitable Jesus' setting his face, not back toward the wilderness, but toward Jerusalem, when all is said and done. Jerusalem's historical destruction in 70 A.D. is anticipated in the Gospels by the transfer of language about Zion in the Old Testament to Jesus in the New — the place of God's full dwelling, a tabernacle not made with human hands. This convergence is further enhanced by the evangelists' depiction of the temple curtain being torn in two at the hour of Jesus' death.

This having been said, old hopes associated with Zion and the city Jerusalem are not just shunted off onto Jesus and spiritualized. They retain their own integrity and remain central to Christian hope. In John's final vision the old temple is gone — the rivers that make glad the city of God flow now from the throne of the Lamb rather than Zion (Rev. 22). But we're back in the heavenly Jerusalem — not Eden, not some bucolic substitute, with cities in the meantime demonized. There in the Revelation to John the entire cast of characters from Israel's scriptures is called back for one final scene: the heavenly Jerusalem and her eternal foe, Babylon; the serpent; the Lamb; the Father; and the saints vindicated, as the deceiver of the whole world is finally and forever destroyed.

"Stay in *the city*," the risen Lord had said in Luke 24:49, "until you are clothed with power from on high." This promise is fulfilled in short order when the Spirit is poured out on "devout men from every nation under heaven dwelling in Jerusalem" (Acts 2:5). In Jerusalem a gift of hearing reverses Babel's confusion of tongues. And all this serves as a foretaste of the final victory in the heavenly Jerusalem, come down to earth at last, as the Spirit poured out in Jerusalem now testifies to John on Patmos. My Old Testament ears are reminded of Ezekiel receiving by the Spirit a vision of Jerusalem's coming glory, her full holiness restored, on the banks of the Chebar. The glory of the LORD departs the Holy City and takes up residence on the mountains to the east — but only in preparation for a glorious return. Now is a time of testing and cleansing and repentance, "that they might know that I am the LORD." The man with the measuring line who describes the new temple in Ezekiel returns in John's revelation, in preparation for the new Jerusalem (Rev. 21).

It should be noted in passing that the hopes associated with Jerusalem are not handed over to some other city — for example, a rival temple at Qumran, or the Samaritans' Mt. Gerizim. This could well have happened, making Rome, Constantinople, Canterbury, Geneva, or Wittenburg the center of biblical hope. Instead, that original hope and language extends to them all, with Jerusalem the original and the others mere facsimiles. Pentecost witnesses to a transfer of God's Spirit from Zion to Jesus, and from Jerusalem to all cities, leaving Rome a mere stage on the journey to all other cities, including the grand metropolis of New York. The church faces the same challenge in this and every city post-Pentecost — caught between the lures of Babylon on one side and the promises of the heavenly Jerusalem on the other.

How a reflection on Jerusalem's destiny throughout the Old and New Testaments might help us understand the church's role in the city today may not at first glance be obvious. And I am wary of making biblical texts do a turn on a dance floor where they do not belong, squeezing out relevance in an artificial way. Still, persistent interest is shown in Jerusalem as the city of God's purposes, directly and indirectly, from beginning to end in Christian Scripture. We cannot renege or spiritualize this fact or set up a rival. A systematic overview is therefore warranted.

But let me confess. This is a huge and sprawling task, and I have wrestled hard with how to get a handle on the topic while respecting the Bible's own specific portrayal. To say the Bible is interested in Jerusalem and Babylon, from beginning to end, as well as evil and suffering in relationship to them both, is not the same thing as producing a blueprint for how the church might take guidance from this for its life today. No one text on the city summarizes them all; yet all of them together do not produce a neatly unfolding or uniform picture. At the same time, the very general title I have chosen does not reflect indecision but a preference for reflecting on the canon's wider sweep rather than on this or that individual text. By using the phrase "Christian Scripture" I also mean to avoid an approach that sets the Testaments up developmentally, or that treats either the Old or the New Testament as containing information from the past that is interesting but requires updating, demythologizing, recalibration, and so forth. By "Scripture" I mean texts that mean to teach me, constrain me, reconstruct my vision of the real, by attention to their plain sense and by illumination of the Spirit, as this was given the prophets and apostles in their own day.

One of the things that will emerge is the persistence and radicality of evil in the biblical depiction. By that I mean this: to the degree that holiness manifests itself in Jerusalem, there is threat in equal measure. We get no further than the second psalm before "the nations conspire, and the peoples of the earth plot in vain" — against the LORD, his anointed, and his holy hill in Jerusalem. Be prepared for a discussion of the city that will sound apocalyptic at times — for that is what my own reflection on the biblical witness has turned up, to a degree I did not anticipate.

If I were to state a thesis at the outset, it would run something like this. The city Jerusalem is the central place where God's presence is known on earth and the residence of God's messiah, David and his offspring. The city and messiah sin and are judged through the agency of Babylon. This sets in motion a force of evil that had once been contained, or had remained on the far horizon of God's dealings with his people Israel. At the same time, ironically, God's judgment on Jerusalem through Babylon has the effect of opening up Jerusalem as the earthly goal "to which the nations shall go up" — all God's people, first the scattered Israel, and then all the nations, who would in time come to bring tribute and worship the One God there; those who were exiled accompanied by their exilers and others. In the words of Zechariah,

> "In those days ten men from the nations of every tongue shall take hold of the robe of a [Judean], saying, 'Let us go with you, for we have heard that God is with you.'" (Zech. 8:23)

Or Isaiah,

> "They will make supplication to you, saying: 'God is with you only and there is no other, no god besides him.'" Truly, thou art a God who hidest thyself, O God of Israel, the Savior. (Isa. 45:14)

If the sons of Abraham were to be the means by which God's blessing would be experienced by all people, the place of that experience in time becomes the city Jerusalem, where God dwells and is not hidden, but makes himself known. Yet frustrating this is a primordial evil force, larger than individual human sin and disobedience, represented by Babylon in the Old Testament and by Satan in the New, both represented in primordial time by the snake and the tower builders of Babel.

In the New Testament, Jesus becomes the place of God's habitation, as Isaiah's star moves from Jerusalem to stop over the place where the infant Messiah was born. Tribute is brought by the nations, Isaiah's gold and frankincense, as once this was to be brought to Zion, by kings drawn "to the brightness of [Zion's] rising" (Isaiah 60:3, 6). Jesus becomes the means by which all nations are blessed, taking up and filling to the full the role of the suffering Zion by his death on Calvary, and filling Zion's role even to overflowing by routing Death and Satan — the primal forces threatening Zion, the floods that lift up their voice, the thundering of many waters requiring a mighty bulkhead. This is followed by the gift of the Spirit at Pentecost, again poured out from the same place of God's glory, Jerusalem. The temple curtain torn in two (Luke 23:45) foreshadows the temple's destruction and the end of its cultic rounds. Strife emerges between the new people of God and the old, as was foreseen by Isaiah, and both are cast adrift in a hostile world as diaspora people. The New Testament insists that Satan has fallen from heaven as once Babylon descended to Sheol in the Old Testament, but the aftershocks of their reign on earth are still felt. In Isaiah there is conflict within Zion after the restoration, and the New Testament testifies to struggles within the church and without, as the church spreads from Jerusalem into every city on earth.

My approach to reading Christian Scripture on this topic is explicitly typological. Here I am simply following the lead of the New Testament, which sees in the old types of God's dealings how they have been filled to the full and to overflowing in Christ. As such, they retain their capacity to teach, after Pentecost and before the Eschaton, and to display for our guidance the life of the people of God, among whom we are now included. As such, we can expect to see in Zion's destiny something of the destiny of every city in which the church, the dwelling place of God's Holy Spirit, finds itself. This involves, as we learn from Zion, obedience and repentance, suffering (sometimes unmerited), assaults from Babylon, and conflicts within and beyond our own struggling number. Yet the hopes for Zion's full restitution — including now those of us modeled on her — are undiminished, because these hopes are grounded in promises from God, bound and sealed in the Old Testament and retaining their force until the vision of Scripture's final book comes to pass. These promises do not rely on unaided human striving but on disciplined service and waiting, because they derive from God himself and are meant to guide and comfort us until he comes again. These statements of hope constitute our own source of life as the church in the city, as we await a time when all peoples will at last come together to worship God, when Satan and Babylon will finally be defeated forever, and when the Messiah will reign as Lord over all.

In Zion, then, we see a foretaste of what is to take place in every city in the Christian dispensation. Zion is not just God's city of old but, as Revelation reminds us, our own hope and final destiny, as the heavenly city descends and takes up unto itself every city on earth.

That, in a nutshell, is my working perspective. Now we will proceed to its slower evolution, from Old Testament to New, each Testament typologically informing the other, neither one coming first or last, both witnessing to Christ and the city Jerusalem, each in its own idiom.

Four aspects of being the church in the city will come to the fore: (1) the need to take seriously threats from the evil within us and above us that can only be addressed with repentance and worship and trust in the Victorious One; (2) the necessity of bearing unmerited suffering, because the poor and helpless in the city are representations of ourselves, needful of the Savior's victory over evil, as we know ourselves to feel that need; (3) the need for persistence through ongoing conflict *within the church itself,* as the aftereffects of Babylon's power and thrall remain forces to reckon with; and (4) the need for a discipline of trust that our city's destiny is God's concern, because the promises lavished on Zion of old have been transferred to the church *wherever* she finds herself, but especially in the city. Revelation's promise of the heavenly Jerusalem is not pie-in-the-sky dreaming, but the conviction born of the Spirit that God is coming toward us to bring to fruition his plans for a new creation, just as we work through prayer and repentance and suffering and persistence to greet him.

*   *   *

I first want to look in general terms at how the city is depicted in the Old Testament. The path I will take leads from the ideal city, Jerusalem, to city building in general, as this is described in the primeval history, in Genesis 1–11. Special attention is paid to the Tower of Babel story at its conclusion. Then the line that clearly connects Babel to Babylon is followed, taking us to Isaiah, where we again encounter God's special city Jerusalem, now pitted against the mighty Babylon. Because the war between Zion and Babylon — seen in Isaiah 13–14; 21; 24–27; 46–47

— is so clearly a type for the battle between Christ and Satan, Isaiah will form the center of our reflection on being the church in the city. Reading Isaiah in this way, one understands why the church fathers called Isaiah the "first apostle," and why Ambrose told the newly converted Augustine that Isaiah is the best place to hear the gospel of Jesus Christ. It is my hope that we, too, will hear the gospel in Isaiah, where Zion plays so central a role and offers a glimpse of the city's destiny in our own dispensation post-Pentecost.

In Israel, Jerusalem is the city where God dwells. His presence is described as *kabod*, glory, effulgence, filling the tabernacle in the temple, a holiness before which all is unclean, even the most righteous of prophets. His presence is also known through his chosen agent of justice, his son, the messiah or anointed one, David and his offspring up to and including the Messiah, Jesus. The relationship between messiah, Lord, and city is not bullet-proof but is open to changes and chances. God can actually absent himself, with the city still intact: so Ezekiel watches God's glory depart from Jerusalem *before* the city is destroyed. Or the messiah can be absent, or meriting judgment, with God's presence in Jerusalem untouched. Or the messiah can be both present and a proper agent of God's *mishpat* without specific attachment to a place. So God promises to David that his lineage will stand forever (2 Sam. 7:12) before he takes up the request to build in Jerusalem "a house for my name."

At the same time, it is clear that God's intention in the fullest sense is for all three — city, messiah, and divine presence — to cohere in such a way that blessing is felt through all creation. "Great is the LORD and greatly to be praised in the city of our God! His holy mountain . . . is the joy of all the earth" (Ps. 48:1-2). The promise of an eternal lineage for David is completed with the promise of an actual physical house, in Jerusalem. The choice of Zion as God's dwelling place, the psalmist insists, includes the Davidic messiah: "I have set my king on Zion, my holy hill" (Ps. 2:6). As the psalm continues, the anointed one is addressed as God's own son: "today I have begotten you." Assaults on the LORD are assaults on his anointed, his messiah. The Ezekiel who watches God's glory depart and whose opinion of anointed shepherds is most cautious also envisions God replanting his messiah, "the topmost cedar sprout," again on Mount Zion, "that it may bring forth boughs and bear fruit, and become a noble cedar; . . . in the shade of its branches birds of every sort shall nest" (Ezek. 17:22-23). However subsequent history conspired against the promises for David, the original promises and promises reissued after the destruction of Jerusalem, these promises are not withdrawn. Following Ezekiel's lead, they are often expanded: God's messiah is to be the sign of God's rule and protection for all peoples. The shoot from the stump of Jesse means nothing less than that "the earth shall be full of the knowledge of the LORD as the waters cover the sea" (Isa. 11:9). To Jerusalem all the nations will stream, "for out of Zion shall go forth the law, and the word of the LORD from Jerusalem" (Isa. 2:3). What the psalmist stated in terms of warning at the beginning, "be warned, O rulers of the earth. Serve the LORD with fear, with trembling kiss his feet" (Ps. 2:10-11), at the end he strains to express in language of praise, extended through all creation: "Let everything that breathes praise the LORD!" (Ps. 150:6).

The mature history of Israel could in fact be traced by attending to this fragile but critical symbiosis: city, messiah, Lord. Jerusalem is the city where God is present and where justice is to go forth and benefit all cities, in Israel and eventually in all the earth. If she did not have that status to begin with, after Zion's Babylonian defeat that increasingly is her role: navel of the universe, destination of all peoples, with the health of the entire cosmos dependent on her. The bulk of the psalms, especially those in the triple digits, have this as their sole theme. "There is a river that makes glad the city of God, the holy habitation of the Most High. God is in the midst of her; she shall not be moved" (Ps. 46:4-5). "The LORD is great in Zion, he is exalted over all the peoples" (99:2). "Let this be recorded for a generation to come . . . that men may declare in Zion the name of the LORD, and in Jerusalem his praise, when peoples gather together, and kingdoms, to worship the LORD" (102:18, 21-22). "Those who trust in the LORD are like Mount Zion, which cannot be moved, but abides for ever" (125:1). I could easily spend the rest of my time doing nothing but quoting from the psalms on this theme.

So why is this divine intention for the holy city — the city of cities — frustrated? It bears repeating that there is nothing inherently flawed about cities in the Bible. Cities are not set in contrast to the country. When did Israel murmur? In the country, where the rule of the road is wild beasts, lack of food, snares and pits.

Cities are depicted as being built no sooner than the paint had dried on the flaming sword guarding Eden. There is no sustained period of country living that then devolves into city life. The first city is built by Cain in Genesis 4 and named after his son. It represents the desire for protection and shelter, for oneself and in the name of one's children. The city has no name, no other purpose, than that. The same Hebrew word, *'ir*, applies to foreign cities and cities in the promised land, cities big and small, holding potential for blessing (Jersualem) or curse (Sodom).

Still, it seems that because city building can get one a name, can serve as a manifestation of human strength, there is the potential for particular evil, of a different sort than what Israel would eventually experience in the wilderness. Cities are mentioned as being built or already in existence shortly after Cain's modest and necessary construction in Genesis 4. Following the flood, the nations emerge from the sons of Noah, and begin to spread out. Cities are built for them. Anticipating the tower of Babel story, Genesis 10 reports the specific building of cities in Assyria and the land of Shinar — that is, Babylonia. Babel, Erech, Akkad, Nineveh, Rehoboth-Ir, and Calah, the great city, are all built by Nimrod in Genesis 10. He is the first on earth to be a *gibbor*, a Schwarzeneggar whose power is tinged with violence. Nimrod is a mighty hunter, the pithy note at Genesis 10:9 reads; to hunt is to be more powerful than animals, to subdue nature. Cities and civilization entail the subjugation of nature. For this Nimrod is renowned. And there is no romantic memory of savage innocence here, an unspoiled time before civilization, Rousseau's lost Eden, just a matter-of-fact description of the movement from one period to the next.

These early Genesis stories, before God calls Abraham, are about the establishment of limits, painful but necessary, and in the end beneficial. Exposed are the limits within which blessing can be experienced: in sexual relationship, in social relationship, in knowledge, in the desires of the heart, in human ambition, and in human labor. Round and round these themes the stories in Genesis 1–11 circle.

Cities are monuments to human labor. They provide shelter, from one generation to the next. But they can also get tied up with the wrong sort of human ambition. To make a name for oneself is not wrong in itself. But in Genesis 11, the final episode in primordial time, city building is connected by the citizens of Babel with an effort to thwart God's designs. This can be the only explanation for the story's curious placement, *after* scattering has occurred and languages have emerged. Yet the citizens propose: "Come, let us build ourselves a city, and a tower with its top in the heavens, and let us make a name for ourselves, lest we be scattered abroad upon the face of the whole earth" (Gen.

11:4). The connection between making a name for oneself and not wanting to be spread abroad, otherwise unclear, is explicable as wanting to undo what God has previously wrought. That it is God's will that humanity scatter, and not a judgment, is made clear by the preceding chapter, where the nations emerge with different languages and identities after the flood in fulfillment of the command to be fruitful and multiply, to fill the earth and subdue it. You recall that this was our only original charge from God in Genesis 1:28: to fill the earth and subdue it. Babel's citizens want to subdue, but on their own terms and not those imposed by the original charge.

The Babel story, the final episode before the call of Abraham, means to take another run at why humanity is scattered and possesses different tongues — not because this was the logical outcome of dispersion and naturalization over time, as God intended, but because there had been an instinct in the human heart connecting labor with making a name through unity of purpose, unfrustrated by language barriers. And with this came an unfortunate catalyzing — depicted as a raid on heaven itself. How these various distinct elements — making a name, grand achievement, not wanting to spread abroad, unity of language and purpose — are logically connected is left unclear by the narrator. But at some point God is forced to conclude, "this is only the beginning of what they will do; and *nothing* that they propose to do will now be impossible for them" (11:6).

What the story reveals is that an element of devising emerges in the wake of human success, which is in the nature of things set against the will of God. Cities, because they contain populations in compression, have the capacity for mobilizing energies and diversities toward a common goal, and at some point accomplishment itself breeds "devices and desires" in the human heart; we may remain unconscious of these things, but they constitute an affront to God, and a threat to true human thriving as he intends it. The successful project intrudes between God and humanity precisely as it takes on a life of its own; it is externalized (the magnificent tower) and then serves as a point of reference for humans beyond simple naming. Ironically, as the story leaves it, as a result of their attempt to make a name for themselves, the citizens of Babel remain forever anonymous. This capacity to externalize human labor into something monumental distinguishes humanity from nature, but it also brings with it a false form of name-seeking, through identification by human projection rather than by God's address. So God confuses all this, leaving even simple names incomprehensible and strange across language groups.

Why this must be so is as unclear as why there is a tree from which we must not eat, whose very prohibition is the source of its appeal. The problem with city building is that no one can tell exactly when the appropriate need for protection and justice and organization slides over into name seeking, human endeavor in love with itself, and a false sense of independence and unity, achieved rather than granted. The story warns about this danger and lets the example of Babel stand as a signpost.

Yet that isn't the end of it. The flaming sword that turns every which way, guarding the tree of life, closes off a period of existence forever. But in Babel we are clearly meant to see Babylon. Here we have an obvious leak into real time and space, and the destiny of a real city. When Babylon the Great then appears in history, there is the distinct possibility that the tower the citizens left off building will be tackled again with fresh mortar and up-to-date plans. A lesson learned could have two outcomes: stop, or try again, wiser and more bent on success than ever.

By contrast, consider Sodom and Gomorrah. These cities, too, are mentioned in Genesis 10, alongside Babylon. For whatever reason, they are not described as having been built but simply appear in the narrative. Their ultimate fate is described in history, tied up with the destiny of Abram's uncle Lot and his family, as well as that of the Moabites and Ammonites. Still, after the destruction of Sodom and Gomorrah reported at Genesis 19, their names are only a byword, recalling a fate from the distant past intended to serve as a warning in the present. Babylon, on the other hand, emerges again on the canvas of history at a much later date, intertwined with Israel's fate, as a replacement for the mighty Assyrians. No Pharaoh, not even the nameless tyrant who refused to let God's people go, ascends as high as Babylon's height. In all the registers of oracles against foreign nations in the prophets of the Old Testament, Babylon's position remains sure, highest of the high. Above the cedars of Lebanon, according to Isaiah, there is Babylon: "You said in your heart, 'I will ascend to heaven; above the stars of God I will set my throne on high.'" And then the kicker: "I will make myself like the Most High" (Isa. 14:13-14). The brief glimpse at Babel's incomplete tower prepares us in primordial time for an evil that will wreak havoc on all creation, not just on an about-to-be-scattered few.

Assyria and Babylonia are frequently conflated in the Old Testament, yet their identities are safeguarded and distinct, just as we know the difference between the Nineveh of Jonah and Nahum and the Babylon of Isaiah and Daniel. When they are closely related, as in Isaiah and Habakkuk, this is because the one is viewed as a foreshadow or advance guard of the other. This is a cause for despair in Habakkuk, as the prophet watches God dispatch Babylon, the bitter and hasty nation whose justice proceeds from itself, on an ironic mission of judgment against Assyria. In Isaiah, it is a simple fact of history, as Assyria, rod of God's fury sent against a godless nation, is replaced and then upstaged by Babylon. In both cases, there is the clear paradox of a world judgment being executed by the epitome of injustice and pride and violence.

I mention Jonah in passing, and it is worth remembering that a better example of the unforgiveable being forgiven, the unrepentant turning from wickedness in order to live, would have sent the reluctant prophet packing for Babylon rather than Nineveh. Yet this is exactly what distinguishes these two superpowers. In Babylon there is a display of evil and violence so rank it cannot be forgiven, because it feeds on its very status as unforgiveable. To come to terms with Babylon outside of primordial time is to approach a proud tower of redoubled effort, which God allows to stand, and which he must limit in a way other than simple scattering. It is important to understand how Babylon is not Nineveh, nor Sodom, whose only vestige is salt pillars and a whiff of sulpher. Particularly as depicted in Isaiah, Babylon emerges as the inverse of Zion, several stages out beyond Assyria, who began as the *just* rod of God's fury, a role Babylon never had.

Let me reconnect with my opening remarks at this point. I believe we should understand the modern city as thriving under the same conditions set forth for God's own place of habitation, Zion, yet now in the dispensation of the Messiah who has come and who will return to judge the world. It is crucial to see in the earlier dispensation of Israel exactly where the threat to God's city comes from and what it looks like. What we glimpse as threatening human thriving in the Babel story we see in mature and full-blown form in Babylon. To talk about being the church in the city without coming to terms with the large-scale forces seeking to undermine the church's presence in the city would be foolhardy. There is an irrational, transpersonal force, illustrated by the biblical Babylon, that runs roughshod over unaided goodwill or human projects for self-reform. The church's first job is therefore to preach the gospel, aware that pitted against it are inevitable principalities and powers. To call on the name of Jesus is to address the only one capable of routing those forces, within and outside the church, in ways that transcend our comprehension. The church in the city without the Messiah is as doomed as Zion before Babylon's might.

Stanley Hauerwas can urge that the church not just have a social ethic but be a social ethic, yet even this distinction pales if one is thinking only about the church pressing its cause on neutral territory, through initiatives of action or simple presence or good works. There is an Enemy pitted against the church that takes up residence in the human heart, and it is likely to be more interested, as Luther reminded us, in the godly than the ungodly. No territory is neutral. The church's first activity is therefore repentance; its second is worship and praise. The Enemy hates all three because they do not represent earthly mobilizations on behalf of this or that just cause, where the slings and arrows of ambition and achievement invade and infect. Instead, by primary attention to the unclean human heart, we arc constantly reminded that we do those things we ought not to do and leave undone what we ought to have done, because that is the naked human condition. All social action flows from prayer addressed to God, mindful of the power of sin and the devil. The cleansing of sin and the crushing of the devil are wholly God's act in Christ, the only one capable of defeating the Babylon pitted against Zion, the only one capable of turning flawed human endeavor into the means of grace and hope of glory, for ourselves and for those we seek to serve in Christ's name. "Simon, behold, Satan demanded to have you, that he might sift you like wheat, but I have prayed for you" (Luke 22:31-32). The church in the city stands or falls by this prayer.

In short, if one sets out to track the city in Christian Scripture, one will in time come upon Babylon, a city that continually presents a threat to all cities — just as Zion and Messiah, on the flip-side, represent and offer hope and life and victory. The tower of Babylon is nothing but the logical culmination of human pride and ambition, such as we saw it in primordial time and witness it in all times and places, allowed by God to go its perilous and all-consuming way.

Isaiah depicts Babylon's defeat, at the same time he depicts a battle so devastating and horrendous as to frustrate simple connection with any moment in past history. "Behold the LORD will lay waste the earth and make it desolate, and he will twist its surface and scatter its inhabitants. . . . The earth shall be utterly laid waste and utterly despoiled; for the LORD has spoken this word" (Isa. 24:1, 3). Here we see the inner nerve of the book of Isaiah: more than any other prophetic book, events are typologically fraught — that is, they mean what they mean for contemporaries but also contain within themselves a significance that has ramifications in the future. There is dramatic movement within the book: Assyria gives way to Babylon; Babylon is defeated by Cyrus; Israel goes home and Zion is restored. Yet by coming into contact with this agent of judgment, Babylon, forces are unleashed upon the cosmos that turn a defeat by Cyrus, however impressive in its day, into something provisional, a foreshadowing of a yet greater battle between forces that can only be called principalities and powers. Chapters 24–27 describe such a battle. A neat connection between justice and protection, righteousness and blessing was broken, and into the vacuum came mighty Babylon. The aftermath is then anything but neat. The raw power that is unleashed creates ripples throughout history, within but also beyond Isaiah's own literary horizon.

So we come to the second aspect of being the city, exemplified by Zion's plight, once Babylon has been permitted to unleash a judgment more awful and more ungodly than Assyria's. Zion must suffer. Chapter 47 tells of Babylon's terror. "You showed [my people] no mercy; . . . you made your yoke exceedingly heavy" (47:6); "secure in your wickedness, you said, 'No one sees me'; . . . 'I am, and there is no one besides me'" (47:10). Even the LORD's own "I am who I am" is here preempted by Babylon. In God's dealing with Israel's sins through such a vile worker of judgment, there was spillage, and Zion bears the brunt of it.

To be the church in the city is to bear a degree of unmerited suffering. Zion has sinned and for that endures punishment, but in addition she suffers on behalf of her children. "For your transgressions," the prophet tells Zion's citizens, "your mother was put away" (Isa. 50:1). To be the church in the city is to take up a cross, simply because Babylon's fury persists and catches in its thrall those who misuse power and in so doing injure the helpless. Because cities are locations of amassed resources and raw power, proud towers are built, which often fall on the innocent. The church is that place where we acknowledge our capacity to generate evil and inflict pain and extend Babylon's legacy. It takes the Messiah's victory to stop the cycle of sin and guilt, and this frees us to attend to innocent suffering and the hurt we ourselves have caused. This is certainly a chief vocation for the church in the city: as the suffering Zion, to see in the poor and helpless Babylon's victims, and yet the rescued of Christ, in the same way we know that rescue has given us new life and hope.

In the book of Lamentations the identification by the author with the suffering Zion reveals a broken and contrite heart — "How lonely sits the city . . . she weeps bitterly in the night. . . . Is it nothing to you, all you who pass by? Look and see if there is any sorrow like my sorrow" (Lam. 1:1, 2, 10) — a heart prepared by God to identify with and serve the poor, not out of general human decency, but because the suffering Zion foreshadows the king who carried his own cross to die in order to break open hearts to imitate and serve him.

It is striking that at this junction of the book of Isaiah, Israel's messiah is missing. Zion bears the suffering for her wayward children, and double for all her own sins. Next to Zion is the nameless Man of Sorrows, who works atonement for those who confess his suffering and death to be an expiation for their sins, while for Babylon "there is no savior" (Isa. 47:15). The remainder of the book speaks of God's intention to save Zion and restore her children to her, to be joined now by the nations. But this intention is frustrated, now as much within as without. Zion's period of intense suffering and humiliation is over, but in its wake comes a different threat: fighting among God's own people, the righteous servants of God buffeted by those in their own midst. All this frustrates and postpones God's return to Zion, and her promised exultation as the place where all nations will worship. Yet the prophet never gives up hope. "Arise, shine; for your light has come, and the glory of the LORD has risen upon you. . . . nations shall come to your light, and kings to the brightness of your rising. . . . They shall bring gold and frankincense, and shall proclaim the praise of the LORD" (Isa. 60:1, 3, 6b). What the prophet here strains to see, the gospel proclaims as having arrived. Jesus is the missing Messiah, the suffering and the resplendent Zion, the Man of Sorrows, and the Victorious Victim.

The coming of the nations — those of us who are not of the household of Israel — is accomplished through Christ, the New Jerusalem, the embodied place where God's Spirit resides and is poured forth. As in Isaiah, this creates tension within Israel, as those outside are brought near. "The shepherds also have no understanding; they have all turned to their own way, each to his own gain, one and all" (Isa. 56:11). But it is a tension that is not so fundamental as to stand in the way of God's final design for all creation: his plan that it be restored and renewed, and that all which divides us be overshadowed by and through our common worship. Just as there is conflict between the new and the old Israel in Isaiah, just as this conflict creates a special tension within the original people of God themselves, so too the church must now experience conflict and tension within its own ranks. This is the third reality facing the church in the city: the presence of conflict within the community. We are not to be caught off guard by this, nor are we to long for a unity that may mask a tower-building desire, or the hope of getting that one single language without any confusion that tells us we've got it all right at last — which could be a raid on heaven, rather than a healthy God-given concern. On the other side, the challenge is how to interpret rightly the conflict that emerges, and not simply welcome conflict as the sign of healthy diversity, until Christian believing has no excluding form whatsoever, and devolves into sentimentality.

In Isaiah, this tension, on the positive side, has to do with the birth pangs caused as Zion gathers to herself, in Christ, children she did not know she had. But Isaiah insists that there will be room. "Enlarge the place of your tent, and let the curtains of your habitations be stretched out; hold not back, lengthen your cords and strengthen your stakes" (Isa. 54:2). Yet this is not an orgy of inclusion *for its own sake*. Much of the conflict we witness in the last eleven chapters of Isaiah is born of an assault on God's holiness in Zion, and idolatry, and false worship, which leads not to inclusion but to destruction for those within and outside the community of faith. For the synagogue, the forbidding last line of Isaiah — which describes those who have rebelled against God everlastingly in eternal fire — is rendered less final by reading after it the verse that precedes it: "all flesh shall come to worship before me, says the LORD" (Isa. 66:23). But even so this does not keep the community unaware that conflict and diversity are never goods unto themselves; when God's holiness is offended against and inclusion leads to false worship, the judgment of God is absolute. There can be no "celebration" of conflict, even though conflict may well witness to the bringing about of God's plans in spite of human sin and offense. Diversity is no good unto itself, even as human distinction is not erased but transformed through the worship of one God, in one place, where the victorious Messiah is now eternally enthroned, because he is that throne in himself.

The last word of Isaiah is not its penultimate verse but the Spirit's gift to John on Patmos, the book of Revelation, which is more indebted to Isaiah than to any other of Israel's scriptures. There Isaiah's unfinished business is concluded. The true last line is supplied. Isaiah's war of judgment on earth had its counterpart in heaven, we learn in Revelation 13. As Babylon's descent in Isaiah was foreshadowed in primordial time by the throwing down of Babel's proud tower, the war in heaven shows the Lamb victorious over the foe from all eternity. End-time and primordial time turn out to be wound on the same clock. In the fourteenth chapter the Lamb appears on Mount Zion, and an angel announces as final what seemed in Isaiah only provisional: "Fallen, fallen is Babylon the great" (14:8). Chapter 18 is an encomium to this defeat, woven from God's words of old to Isaiah. In the remaining chapters of Revelation, the saints who have endured and those who have died in the LORD together witness the great city Jerusalem coming down out of heaven for her long-promised exultation, with the Messiah himself not just her throne but her temple, the source of living and healing water for all nations.

John knows that we are living between the times and must now endure. But our hope is sure. We see our destiny in that of Zion, and the Spirit has testified to God's own purpose at work to reward the saints. It is that hope by which we live in times of evil assault, suffering, and conflict whose issue is not ours to know, except as that is given to us by him who has conquered evil before the foundations of the world and calls us to be faithful in the middle time. Let the risen Lord's word to the disciples be our own, in this middle time: "'Behold, I send the promise of my Father upon you; but stay in the city, until you are clothed with power from on high.' . . . And they returned to Jerusalem with great joy, and were continually in the temple blessing God" (Luke 24:49, 52).

Resist the evil one; endure suffering; persist through conflict; trust him whose city this is. Above all, imitate Christ — who imitated Zion in suffering and in holiness and made her the city God finally intended. In this way the church will be the holy city within the city until Christ comes again to redeem the faithful and the heavenly Jerusalem comes down to claim its eternal citizens.

"With His own blood He bought her, and for her life He died."

Augustine's City of God Today

ROBERT L. WILKEN

Reading the Scriptures as an old man, St. Augustine was drawn to the historical books of the Bible. After he was ordained priest he had studied the epistles of St. Paul; later as a bishop he preached a series of sermons on the Gospel of John and wrote a long commentary on the book of Psalms. But in the last years of his life he found himself rereading the history of the kings of Israel recorded in the books of Samuel and the books of Kings. What impressed him most in these books, Peter Brown observes in his biography of Augustine, "was the manner in which the hidden ways of God had caused the most reasonable policies to miscarry."[1]

The dream that human beings, guided by reason and tempered by virtue and goodwill, could build an enduring city in this world was no less the hope of men and women in ancient times than it is in our own time. For many it seemed that this hope had been realized in the accomplishments of the Roman Empire. No other political order had been so successful in embracing so many peoples in so many different countries in one system of government. Even today one can gaze at the ruins of Roman cities from one end of the Mediterranean world to the other, in Tunisia, in Turkey, in Syria, and marvel that they all were once part of a single rule, a common culture, one world. Rome was unique. It could not only boast of stability and prosperity and the rule of law; it claimed universality. And it aspired to finality. It was known as the eternal city, "Roma Aeterna," a city

1. Peter Brown, *Augustine of Hippo* (Berkeley: University of California Press, 1967), p. 423.

28

that would endure long after others had fallen. As Virgil, the great poet of the Roman Empire, sang, for the Romans the gods "set no limits, world or time/But make the gift of empire without end" (*Aeneid* 1:374-75). As long as there is human life, Rome would endure.

As a boy Augustine had committed Virgil's lines to memory. He was raised with the knowledge that Rome — the city, the institutions that gave stability and order to the provinces of the empire, its language and culture — had been there from time immemorial, and he had been led to expect that what had been received from the past would continue indefinitely. He could no more conceive of Rome passing away than most Americans can conceive that our way of life and institutions might one day pass into oblivion. In one of his sermons he spoke of the "city that had given us birth according to the flesh," to which he added, "Thanks be to God" (*Ser.* 105.9).

Yet he lived at a time when the very institutions that he cherished were threatened. In A.D. 410, when Augustine was in his late fifties, the city of Rome was sacked by a Gothic army that had marched down into Italy from the "barbarian" north. To the horror of the inhabitants of Rome as well as of citizens all over the empire, these barbarians had looted and plundered the city, and with impunity. Rome had stood for a thousand years; never before had she been overrun by a foreign army. Citizens of the Roman Empire were stunned, fearful, incredulous. Although the emperor and his court were now located in Constantinople far to the East, Rome was the titular capital. Rome was more than a city; it symbolized a tradition of civilized rule, a way of life, an ancient culture, permanence and security, the things that make social and civic life possible. "If Rome can perish," wrote Jerome, "what can be safe?" His sentiments were also Augustine's.

The sack of Rome in 410 A.D. was the immediate occasion for Augustine's *City of God*, but the book is much more than a response to that event. It can be read as a Christian response to Plato's *Republic*. There Plato had sketched out a rational ideal of a perfect commonwealth, in Augustine's words, "what kind of city" human beings ought to strive to realize in this world (*Civ.* 2.14.1). Plato does not figure large in the *City of God*; he lurks, however, in the background. Augustine's immediate targets are the Platonists, philosophers such as Plotinus and Porphyry, usually called Neoplatonists, who had defended the traditional gods of the ancient cities. In the very first sentence Augustine says that he has taken upon himself the task of "defending the glorious city of God against those who prefer their own gods to the Founder of that city."

A striking feature of this opening sentence is that Augustine does not say he is defending *belief* in the one God, nor the person of Christ, nor Christian teaching. His book is not a defense of an idea; it is defense of a city, the "city of God." The term "city" designates a community, a corporate and social entity, an ordered, purposeful gathering of human beings. Augustine never defines this city outright, but it is closely identified with the church. *The City of God* was written, he tells us, against philosophers who attack "the city of God, that is [God's] Church" (12.6).

The City of God is a book about the church, and the first thing to learn from Augustine is that Christian thinking about society does not exist independently of what Christians think about the church. Any discussion of the relation of Christianity to the political realm, to culture and society, must begin with that community whose end transcends history. For the coming of Christ brought into being a new kind of community, the church, and it is as members of this fellowship that Christians participate in the life of the political communities in which they live. As Sheldon Wolin put it some years ago:

> The significance of Christian thought for the Western political tradition lies not so much in what it had to say about the political order, but primarily in what it had to say about the religious order. The attempt of Christians to understand their own group life provided a new and sorely needed source of ideas for Western political thought. Christianity succeeded where the hellenistic and late classical philosophies had failed, because it put forward a new and powerful idea of community which recalled men to a life of meaningful participation.[2]

I

Christian thinking on the church and social and political life begins, as does all early Christian thought, with the Bible. To introduce the theme of his book Augustine cites three passages, all from the Psalms: "Glorious things are spoken of you, O city of God" (Ps. 87:3); "Great is the Lord and greatly to be praised in the city of our God" (Ps. 48:1); and "There is a river whose streams make glad the city of God, the holy habitation of the Most High. God is in the midst of her, she shall not be moved" (Ps. 46:4-5; *Civ.* 11.1).

All three of these texts are speaking about Jerusalem, the ancient city in Palestine, the city of Jewish kings and the city where Jesus was killed, a city that one can locate on a map. But for Augustine the phrase "city of God" in these psalms also bore another meaning; it designated the company of men and women who are united in their love of God. His book is about this city; yet Augustine says that to depict the city of God he must speak about another city, "the city of this world," the earthly city, the political and legal institutions that exercise dominion over human beings (1, pref.). The two cities must be discussed in relation to each other because "in this present transitory world, they are inter-woven and mingled with one another" (11.1). The citizens of the city of God are also citizens of the earthly city, and some of the citizens of the earthly city belong to the city of God.

In setting forth the ends of the two cities, Augustine begins with definitions that were well known to Roman political thinkers. He draws on Varro, a Roman philosopher, and Cicero, the great Roman statesmen. In book 2 he cites Cicero's *De Republica*, where Cicero defines a political community not as any association of human beings but as "an association united by a common sense of right and a community of interest" (2.21). But in his most detailed discussion of the ends of the two cities, Augustine starts at another place. He says that the end toward which all human life is directed is "peace." "Anyone who joins me in an examination, however slight, of human affairs, and the human nature we all share, recognizes that just as there is no man who does not wish for joy, so there is no man who does not wish for peace" (19.12). Even when men go to war their aim is to achieve peace. All our "use of temporal things," he writes, "is related to the enjoyment of earthly peace in the earthly city" (19.14).

For Augustine "peace" does not refer simply to external peace — that is, the peace that exists between two peoples or kingdoms who share a common boundary. Peace also applies to the relations between members of a family, to the bond of trust that exists between citizens in a city, the laws that make it possible for citizens to carry on their activities without discord or fear or danger. For Augustine peace means order within society, it presupposes law, and it requires justice. Peace without justice, he writes, "is not worthy even of the name of peace" (19.12). All of the components of society — the family, the city, its legal and political institutions — are directed to a common end, securing and preserving peace.

Augustine realized, however, that "peace" was not simply a word borrowed from the lexicon of political thought. It was also a major term in the Bible, where it is used of the city of God and of peace with God. The passage that caught his attention was from Psalm 147, a psalm that speaks about Jerusalem, the city of God: "Praise the LORD, O Jerusalem! Praise your God, O Zion! For he strengthens the bars of your gates . . . He makes peace within your borders" (147:12-14). This psalm teaches us, says Augustine, that the end of the city of God is "peace." To which he adds, drawing on a traditional etymology of the name Jerusalem, "Jerusalem means city of peace."

As a goal or end, peace applies equally well to the earthly city and to the city of God. This seems puzzling because Augustine has suggested throughout the book that the two cities have different ends. For this reason he introduces another biblical text, this one from St. Paul, that speaks of the "end" of the city of God as "everlasting life." Paul writes: "But now that you have been set free from sin and have become slaves of God, the return you get is sanctification and its end, eternal life" (Rom. 6:22). Augustine will not, however, give up the term "peace," so he settles on the formulation that the "end" of the city of God can be called "peace in life everlasting" or "life everlasting in peace." What sets the city of God off from other communities is that it seeks "the end that is without end" (22.30).

Throughout his discussion Augustine's language is social, not individualistic. Peace does not simply mean union between an individual believer and God; it is a "perfectly ordered and harmonious fellowship in the enjoyment of God, and a mutual fellowship in God." Peace is an end that can only be fulfilled in community and enjoyed when all the members of the community share in that good.

II

Everything that Augustine says about the heavenly city *and* about the earthly city is related to peace. But peace, as Augustine understands it, can never be found in this life, for the peace that human beings are able to create among themselves is always unstable, uncertain, ephemeral. The Scriptures offer no promises concerning peace on this earth. The peace for which the city of God yearns can only be the work of God; it is not built by human hands. Augustine cites the well-known words of the prophet Habakkuk, "The just man lives on the basis of faith" (Hab. 2:4). According to the prophet, the end for which we strive cannot be seen with our eyes, hence we must seek it "by believing." If we are to reach this end "we must be helped" by God, who is that very good which we seek.

In this life it is possible for some human beings to find a measure of peace, but, observes Augustine, we need only look around to see the miseries that can afflict our bodies. "The attitudes and movements of the body, when they are graceful and harmonious . . . , but what if some illness makes the limbs shake and tremble? What if a man's spine is so curved as to bring his hands to the ground, turning the man into a virtual quadruped? Will not this destroy all beauty and grace of body whether in repose or in motion?" No matter what efforts we make to secure a safe haven in life, we cannot avoid being "tossed about at the mercy of chance and accident" (19.4).

What is more, human beings discover that we cannot even find peace within ourselves. The more we strive for virtue, the more we uncover forces within ourselves that work against our best efforts. What stands in the way of a virtuous life is not what comes from outside — for example, the evils of society — but our own vices. Even when we do achieve a measure of goodness in our lives, virtue does not make us immune from suffering or grief. Genuine happiness, happiness that is full and complete, always remains a matter of hope. As St. Paul wrote: "It is in hope that we are saved," which means that in hope we "find happiness" (19.4).

Augustine's argument rests on a theological conviction and an experiential truth. The theological conviction is that happiness can only be found in fellowship with God and with each other in God, for God is the final good toward which human life tends and for whom human beings were created. Because we are made in the image of God our destiny is to live in fellowship with God. The experiential truth is that human life offers no certain and enduring peace, whether it be peace among nations, peace within the city, peace in the home, or peace in the inner chambers of the soul. It is an illusion to think that one can achieve perfect happiness in this life, and it is vain to imagine that human beings can create institutions that will ensure durable peace and stability. The society of which Plato spoke exists only as a matter of discussion among philosophers; it has never existed and cannot exist as an actual human community.

III

Were Augustine's *City of God* to end at this point it would hold much less interest for readers, ancient and modern, than it did and does. What gives his book its fascination and its greatness is that Augustine knew that efforts to achieve peace on this earth, though frail and transitory, must be undertaken. He illustrates this point with one of the most familiar, yet compelling, stories in his book. What shall we say, he asks, about a judge whose office it is to determine the fate of men and women who come before him, knowing all the while that he cannot see into the minds of the people he judges? How can he be certain that his judgment is just? Will he not on occasion condemn an innocent person out of ignorance?

What is the judge to do? Should he, in the absence of indisputable evidence, refuse to judge? Augustine writes: "In view of [the] darkness that attends the life of human society, will our wise man take his seat on the judge's bench, or will he not have the heart to do so?" To which Augustine replies, "He will sit. For the claims of human society constrain him and draw him to this duty; and it is unthinkable to him that he should shirk it."

The claims of human society constrain him! What are these claims? If the ends toward which we strive are always a matter of hope, and peace is a work of God, on what basis does Augustine defend the action of the judge?

To understand his reasoning it may be helpful to set Augustine's thinking in context. For most of its history up to Augustine's day, Christianity was a minority religion in the Roman Empire. Up until the middle of the third century the number of Christians was very small. The sociologist Rodney Stark, on the basis of statistical projections, suggests that by the year 200 there may have been only a little more than 200,000 Christians in an empire of sixty million. By the year 300, however, the number may have risen to over six million. By the time Augustine was born in mid-century the total may have risen to over thirty million. Christians were no longer outsiders; the emperor was a Christian, as were many imperial officials, civic leaders, and magistrates.

For Christians who lived during the first three centuries the task of running the cities and the empire seemed to be someone else's responsibility. Origen of Alexandria, who lived in the early part of the third century, thought that Christians should not hold public office. They served their cities best by offering prayers for those in authority and teaching people to lead lives devoted to God. By our prayers, he writes, "we contribute to the public affairs of the community" (*Cels.* 8.73).

By Augustine's time, however, Christians did not enjoy such luxury. Without the participation of Christians the cities would lack qualified people to serve as magistrates, judges, civic officials, teachers, and soldiers. Among some of Augustine's most interesting letters are those written to civil or military officials who were Christians, men who were no less engaged in preserving the peace of the earthly city than those who were not Christians. They, too, had a stake in the rule of law, in stability, in order, in civic concord, in peace with those peoples who lived outside of the Roman Empire.

Yet as Christians they belonged to a community whose end lay outside of history, and whose company was even larger than the church. Its history extended back into the history of Israel, and it included men and women who had lived in former times, the saints who had gone before; and it awaited others who were not yet born (or already born) who would one day become its citizens. As Augustine was fond of putting it, the church is that part of the city of God which is on pilgrimage "in this condition of mortality and which lives on the basis of faith." Not only the saints who have gone before but also the angels are members of the city of God. In a beautiful phrase Augustine says that the "angels await our arrival" (*En. in ps.* 62.6). The church lived in the company of a much larger community.

It is understandable, then, that Christians thought of themselves as citizens of two cities, the city of God and the earthly city. As citizens of the heavenly city they knew that their deepest yearnings could be satisfied only in loving God, and that peace would be attained only in fellowship with God. Yet in this life, when the city of God is on pilgrimage, its members were full citizens of the communities in which they lived. Like other citizens they were in need of law, of stability, of external concord. For Augustine these goods were not possible without coercion, and he recognized that in this fallen world human beings could not live together without some form of coercion. This is the reason, he writes, for "the power of the king, the power of the sword exercised by a judge, the talon of the executioner, the weapons of the soldier, the discipline of a lord, and the firmness of a good father. All these have their methods, their causes, their reasons, their usefulness. While these are feared, the wicked are kept within bounds and the good live more peacefully among the wicked" (*Ep.* 153.6.16).

As citizens of the earthly city, the citizens of the city of God benefit by the laws and institutions of the earthly city. Yet the Scriptures promise a peace in which there will no longer be the "necessary duty" of ordering society by coercion (19.16). Until we arrive at this state of peace, the citizens of the two cities share certain things in common; they differ, however, in how they use these things. The city of God views everything — laws, ways of ordering societies, social practices and customs — in light of a fuller, more perfect order, never as ends in themselves. It approaches all political institutions as instrumental, as "supports" to aid in bearing the burdens that attend human life. The citizens of the earthly city who have no transcendent point of reference, in contrast, view the peace established by the earthly city as the primary, indeed, the sole end of human life.

The city of God knows it must "make use of earthly and temporal things." For this reason Augustine says that there is a "coming together of human wills," an agreement whereby the citizens of the city of God join with the inhabitants of the earthly city "about things pertaining to mortal life" (19.17). In Augustine's mind this conjunction is always prudential. The customs and practices of society can be embraced as long as they do not mold the souls of the faithful or distract them from their ultimate goal of fellowship with God and with one another in God. "She [the city of God] takes no account of any difference in customs, laws, and institutions by which earthly peace is achieved and preserved" (19.17). Augustine seems to imply that the city of God has *no* interest in the affairs of the earthly city. Yet he adds one qualification, and it is this qualification that gives his book its enduring significance. The city of God, he writes, "neither annuls nor abolishes" the institutions of the society in which she lives "*provided that* no hindrance is presented thereby to the religion which teaches that the one supreme and true God is to be worshipped" (19.17).

At the very point in his discussion where it appears Augustine has drawn a thick line between the affairs of the earthly city and the heavenly city, he injects something unexpected. The city of God *does* have an interest in the affairs of the earthly city — the earthly city must honor and venerate the one true God. The qualifier "provided that" (in Latin *si non*) introduces the one exception, the one claim made on the earthly city. What does Augustine mean?

IV

Early on, Augustine cited a passage from Cicero's *De Republica* about the nature of political communities. The passage read: a people is defined as a multitude "united in association by a common sense of right and a community of interest." The term in this definition used for "right" is *jus*, the word from which the Latin term *justitia* comes, and from which we derive our English word "justice." Augustine explains that Cicero understood this definition to mean that there can be no political community *(res publica)*, no commonwealth, no state "without justice." For where there is no "true justice there can be no *jus*," no law, no equity, no right.

Augustine fastens onto one feature of Cicero's definition of a political community: it must be a community of justice. A republic is not simply a "community of interest"; what gives the community its distinctive character is that it is bound together by *jus*, by law or justice. A community that is united only on the basis of a common interest could just as well be a mob or a gang of pirates. Where there is no justice but only brigandry, lawlessness, and exploitation there is no commonwealth. Justice, however, does not have to do simply with the relation of human beings to one another; it also has to do with God. How can one say that it is unjust for someone to take an estate away from a person who has bought it and give it to someone else, and at the same time say that God is not to be given his due? If one does not serve God, what kind of "justice" can there be? Augustine concludes that a commonwealth that does not serve God cannot be a genuine republic.

Augustine is not speaking here about god in general, about an undefined and amorphous deity; his book is not a defense of a form of ancient deism. The God of which he speaks is the God of the Bible. Some of his critics had asked: Who is this God you talk of and how is it that this is the "only one" to whom the Romans owe obedience?

Augustine answers by reminding his critics that the God of the Bible is well known from the history of Israel (which he has recounted in the *City of God*), from Christ and the church. Hence the only answer at this point in human history to the question "Which God?" must be, "the same God whose prophets foretold the events we now see happening. He is the God from whom Abraham received the message, 'In your descendants all nations will be blessed.' And this promise was fulfilled in Christ, who sprang from that line by physical descent." And, Augustine adds, he is the same God who is acknowledged by Porphyry, the "most learned of philosophers." In sum, the God to whom justice is due is the one and only God, the creator of all things, the God who elected Israel and appeared in Christ. He is the God who commanded sacrifices to be offered "to no other being whatsoever but to himself alone."

The first biblical text to be cited in the *City of God* is Habakkuk 2:4, "the just shall live by faith." In Augustine's Latin this text reads "justus vivit ex fide." The term *justus* (just person) is derived from *jus* and is of course related to *justitia*. This same passage is also cited at the beginning of book 19. What interests Augustine about this text is that it provides a link between the justice that is a necessary mark of a genuine commonwealth and the justice due to God, as exemplified in the just person who lives by faith in the one God. Justice, Augustine says again and again, can only be found where God is worshiped. As a just person lives on the basis of faith, so the "association of just men [and women]" also lives on the basis of faith. Where this justice, the justice due to God, does not exist, there is no commonwealth.

Once Augustine has defined a commonwealth by reference to justice, he proposes yet another definition. He suggests that a "people is the association of a multitude of rational beings united by a common agreement on the objects of their love." The question to be asked of any political community is this: What does it love? This is a characteristically Augustinian, and one might say biblical, way of putting things. What one loves determines what kind of person one is, and what a community loves determines what kind of community it is. If this definition is applied to Rome, says Augustine, it is clear that Rome is a people and that its corporate life *(res)* is indubitably a commonwealth. But it is a very inferior kind of commonwealth because it does not render worship to the one true God. Because Rome does not give God his due, it is a city "devoid of true justice."

Why is this so? Augustine's answer is that the good for which all human beings yearn, the final end of human life, the highest good, is God. It is only in God that human beings find fulfillment and perfection. If they have no sense of God, they have no sense of themselves, a point that is made by John Paul II in *Evangelium Vitae:* "When the sense of God is lost, there is also a tendency to lose the sense of man, of his dignity and his life" (par. 21). Although it may appear that a political community can form its people in virtue without venerating God, in time they will be turned to lesser ends, and hence to vice rather than to virtue. For virtue is not simply a matter of behaving in a certain way; it has to do with attitudes and sentiments as well as deeds, with loves as well as with duties and obligations. Without love of God the virtues cannot bring human beings to perfection, because they have no *telos*, no end toward which they are directed. To live virtuously requires renewing the mind and tutoring the affections as well as disciplining the body. Only in honoring and serving God can human communities nurture genuine virtue. As always, Augustine rests his discussion on an apt scriptural text, again one from the Psalms: "Blessed is the *people* whose God is the LORD" (Ps. 144:15).

The city of God, then, embodies in its own life and worship a fundamental truth about human beings and about society. Only God can give ultimate purpose to our lives. Without God there can be no human fulfillment and no genuine communal life. A society that denies or excludes from its life what makes human beings human — that we are made in the image of God and are restless until we find our rest in God — will be neither just, nor virtuous, nor peaceful. The point is twofold. First, all human life, not just religious life, is directed toward that good which is God, the summum bonum. Hence all our actions come to fulfillment and perfection in the God who is Lord of all and the desire of all human hearts. Second, life directed toward God is always social. Virtue cannot be pursued independently of other human beings. The solitary virtuous person is an anomaly. It is as a "people" that we are blessed.

Augustine offers no theory of political life, but he shows that God can never be relegated to the periphery of a society's life. By discussing the two cities, he is able to draw a contrast between the life of the city of God, a life that is centered on God and genuinely social, and the life of the earthly city that is centered on itself. As Rowan Williams has observed, the *City of God* is a book "about the optimal form of corporate human life in the light of . . . its last end." Augustine wished to redefine the realm of the public to make a place for the spiritual, for God. In his view "it is life outside the Christian community which fails to be truly public, authentically political. The opposition is not between public and private, church and world, but between political virtue and political vice. At the end of the day, it is the secular order that will be shown to be 'atomistic' in its foundations."[3] A society that has no place for God will disintegrate into an amoral aggregate of competing, self-centered interests destructive of the commonwealth. In time it will be enveloped in darkness.

V

It has sometimes been argued that in the *City of God* Augustine makes a place for a neutral secular space where men and women of goodwill can come together to build a just society and culture on the basis of "things relevant to this mortal life." Here there could be a joining of hands of the city of God and the earthly city for the cultivation of the arts of civilization. But for Augustine, a neutral secular space could only be a society without God, subject to the lust for power, the *libido dominandi*. He was convinced that even in this fallen world there could be no genuine justice or peace without the worship of God. Where a people has no regard for God, there can be no social bond, no common life, and no virtue.

Augustine is an apologist neither for a secular public space nor for theism. His book is a defense of the worship of the one true God, the God of the Bible, and of the community that worships and serves this God. The *City of God* is — I repeat — a book about the church. It is only in relation to the church and its destiny that Augustine takes up questions concerning the earthly city. Augustine is interested finally in speaking about God and about life in God, the peace that can only be found in God. Near the end of the book he writes:

> The reward of virtue will be God himself, who gave the virtue, together with the promise of himself, the best and greatest of all possible promises. For what did he mean when he said, in the words of the prophet, "I shall be their God, and they will be my people"? Did he not mean, "I shall be the source of their satisfaction; I shall

---

3. Rowan Williams, "Politics and the Soul: A Reading of the City of God," *Milltown Studies* 19/20 (1987): 58.

be everything that men can honourably desire; life, health, food, wealth, glory, honor, peace and every blessing"? For that is also the correct interpretation of the Apostle's words, "so that God may be all in all." [God] will be the goal of all our longings; and we shall see him for ever; we shall love him without satiety; we shall praise him without wearying. This will be the duty, the delight, the activity of all, shared by all who share the life of eternity. (22.30)

Like other early Christian apologists, Augustine realized that it was not enough to make vague appeals to transcendent goods, to the god of the philosophers, to a deity that takes no particular form in human life. Only people schooled in the religious life can tell the difference between serving the one God faithfully and bowing down to idols. Without such a community the temptation of idolatry is irresistible. For Augustine, defense of the worship of the true God required necessarily a defense of the church, the city of God as it exists in time, on pilgrimage.

The prime example of how God is to be worshiped, and hence of the justice due to God, is the church's offering of itself in the eucharist.

> It is we ourselves — we, his city — who are his best, his most glorious sacrifice. The mystic symbol of this sacrifice we celebrate in our oblations familiar to the faithful. . . . It follows that justice is found where God, the one supreme God, rules an obedient city according to his grace, forbidding sacrifice to any being save himself alone. . . . Where this justice does not exist, there is certainly no "association of men united by a common sense of right and by a community of interests." Therefore there is no commonwealth, for where there is no "people," there is no "weal of the people." (19.23)

The church by offering itself to God as a living sacrifice foreshadows the peace that is everlasting, the "end that is without end," when God will be all in all.

Natural Law in Theology and Ethics

CARL E. BRAATEN

A Statement of the Problem

For the greatest part of the history of Christianity, some type of natural law theory has been used as a bridge to connect the Christian faith and the surrounding culture, the church and the world. In recent times, a deeply entrenched common opinion circulates in church and theology that Protestantism has rejected natural law and thereby distinguishes itself from Roman Catholic moral theology. The body of Roman Catholic social teaching is impressive; but without the recurrent appeal to natural law, the whole body of Catholic moral teaching on labor, industry, and society would lack its spinal column. In contrast, modern Protestantism has no coherent body of social teachings of comparable value and stability.

Abraham Kuyper, the Dutch Reformed theologian, said, on the occasion of the publication of *Rerum Novarum* in 1891: "It must be admitted to our shame that the Roman Catholics are far ahead of us in their study of the social question. Indeed, very far ahead. . . . The action of the Roman Catholics should spur us Protestants to show more dynamism. . . . The Encyclical of Leo XIII gives the principles which are common to all Christians, and which we share with our Roman Catholic compatriots."[1]

1. Abraham Kuyper, *Christianity and the Class Struggle* (Grand Rapids: Piet Hein, 1891), p. 14, note.

A portion of this article was published in *First Things* 19 (January 1992): 20-26, under the title "Protestants and Natural Law."

At the core of the encyclical is an appeal to reason and human nature, but not, of course, without a sure grasp of faith and revealed truth. Natural law is the bridge category used to appeal not only to those who share an *a priori* commitment to sacred Scripture and the Christian creed but to people of all races, classes, cultures, and religions. It is believed that there is one universal natural law to which all people have access by their natural reason, no matter where or when they happen to live.

In much of modern Protestant theology, doubt prevails as to the viability of such an appeal to reason and natural law in Christian social ethics. The bridge has been shattered. So what the churches have to say on social issues has no way of reaching the other side, and the churches end up in dangerous isolation from society, speaking only to themselves.

H. Richard Niebuhr's classic book, *Christ and Culture*,[2] depicts five models of relationship between the church and society. At one extreme are those who set Christ against culture, which leads to a sectarian strategy of withdrawing from the world into separate communities. At the other extreme — Christ of culture — are those who collapse their Christian identity into the cultural *Zeitgeist*, thus becoming culture-conforming Christians. The middle three models represent the typical Catholic, Lutheran, and Calvinist ways of relating Christianity and culture. Catholics have held rather firmly to natural law thinking in constructing their social teachings. The modern representatives of the two branches of the magisterial Reformation, Lutherans and Calvinists, have not so clearly retained a firm foothold in natural law theory. In fact, they swing wildly between a position of utter rejection of natural law and one of conditional acceptance, but they almost never fully concede as much to natural law as we find in modern Catholic social teaching.

I intend to tell the story of the inner Protestant struggle over the question of natural law, from complete rejection in Barthian covenant theology to qualified acceptance in the Lutheran theology of the orders of creation, which draws a proper distinction between law and gospel, creation and redemption. I will conclude with the proposal that Christian social ethics reappropriate the natural law tradition, taking into account the validity of the recent tradition of criticism, and placing natural law carefully within theological brackets defined by principles

2. H. Richard Niebuhr, *Christ and Culture* (New York: Harper & Row, 1956).

articulated in the Reformation tradition, particularly in the Lutheran branch, which I know best, and with an added twist of eschatological theology.

The Rejection of Natural Law in the Protestant Tradition

Karl Barth rejected every form of natural theology and thereby pulled the rug out from under natural law. Only Barth and his friend Eduard Thurneysen among the early dialectical theologians remained consistent and radical in their repudiation of natural law. Others, such as Emil Brunner, Friedrich Gogarten, and Rudolf Bultmann, reopened the door to some new version of natural theology by incorporating philosophy into the theological enterprise. Brunner took the lead in calling for a return to natural theology and natural law,[3] although Barth was able to show that Brunner's position was shot through with ambiguity. The controversy between Barth and Brunner did not settle anything. Some followed Barth in holding that Christian ethics has no use for natural law, which concerns itself with universal principles inscribed in human nature and ascertainable by reason. Instead, Christian ethics is based directly on the command of the living God, which "is always an individual command for the conduct of this man, at this moment and in this situation; a prescription for this case of his; a prescription for the choice of a definite possibility of human intention, decision and action."[4] Here we have the root of Protestant situation ethics, later popularized by Joseph Fletcher and reduced to the absurd in a more humanistic framework.

Barth never provided a systematic treatment of natural law, but throughout his various stages of development he battled against every appeal to natural theology or natural law. As he said, theological ethics that bases itself on the Word of God alone "will not, then, make the disastrous, traitorous use of 'natural' theology, which is the only use that can be made of it."[5] He saw natural law as the self-assertion of auton-

3. Cf. Emil Brunner, *Justice and the Social Order* (New York: Harper & Row, 1945) and *The Divine Imperative* (Philadelphia: Westminster Press, 1947).
4. Karl Barth, *Church Dogmatics,* ed. and trans. Geoffrey W. Bromiley (Edinburgh: T. & T. Clark, 1961), III/4, pp. 11-12.
5. Barth, *Church Dogmatics,* II/2, p. 523.

omous humanity and natural religion, and for this reason he felt he had to speak an irreconcilable no to every attempt to derive ethical norms either from the orders of creation, as Lutherans did, or from nature, as Catholics did.

Barth recognized, of course, that there is such a thing as natural law, in the same sense as he recognized that there is human religion. At its best, natural law is the quest for order on the part of the state and of non-Christians, who have no other source of knowledge, inasmuch as they do not derive their knowledge from above — that is, from divine revelation in Christ and the Bible. The dilemma for Barthian Christians is how it is possible to engage in public ethical discourse in a pluralistic world when the majority, who are non-Christian, do not accept the Christian source of revelation. Barth's refusal to find common ground or an apologetic bridge on which both Christians and non-Christians could walk and talk was not convincing to other theologians — notably Emil Brunner, who resumed an interest in natural law, although always seemingly with something of a bad conscience on account of Barth's strictures.

Barth was not alone in rejecting natural law. Perhaps his most faithful disciple in this area was Jacques Ellul, the French professor of jurisprudence at the University of Bordeaux and author of almost as many books as Karl Barth himself. Ellul wrote a little book called *The Theological Foundations of Law*[6] in which he based all of law and justice on Christology. The claim is an ontological one. The whole world and the entire human situation have changed on account of God's revelation and redemptive act in Christ. Law must also be affected by this event, if it is indeed true. Christians and non-Christians are both objectively in a new situation, since Christ died for all and was raised for the world's justification. Whatever has been called natural law henceforth loses its determinative character and is relativized by justification.

The problem with this thoroughgoing christological basis of natural law is that it is derived from a source that non-Christians do not share. Hence, no bridge, no common ground. Since the majority do not live within the covenant community and do not share its basis, what other basis is there for cooperation between Christians and non-Christians in the public orders of life? We are confronted either by a triumphalist

6. Jacques Ellul, *The Theological Foundations of Law* (London: SCM Press, 1960).

theology of glory in which Christians must conquer the public space
or by sectarian withdrawal into ghetto-like communities alongside of
the world. The hermeneutical issue becomes a burning one. If everything bearing on law and justice is derived from the Bible on account
of Christ and is known exclusively by the community of believers, then
how is it possible for non-Christians to do what is good and right?

The Protestant rejection of natural law has found expression in
American theology in the ethics of Paul Lehmann and Stanley Hauerwas. Paul Lehmann, my professor of ethics at Harvard Divinity School,
renounced natural law theory in the name of his "koinonia ethics."
Following Barth, he rejected the idea "that there is a common link
between the believer and the non-believer grounded in the nature of
human reason which enables both believer and non-believer to make
certain ethical judgments and to address themselves in concert to com-
monly acknowledged ethical situations."[7] Stanley Hauerwas flatly
asserts that "Christian ethics theologically does not have a stake in
'natural law' understood as an independent and sufficient morality."[8]
Ethics stands exclusively on the basis of the story about God that
Christians learn from the Bible within the context of a covenant community.

Protestant Criticisms of Natural Law

Why did the tradition of natural law fall on hard times in Protestant
theology? One might plausibly imagine that the reason lies deeply
embedded in the Reformation theology of Martin Luther and John
Calvin. However, John T. McNeill, the Reformation historian, reached
the following conclusion from his studies:

> There is no real discontinuity between the teaching of the Reformers
> and that of their predecessors with respect to natural law. Not one
> of the leaders of the Reformation assails the principle. Instead, with
> the possible exception of Zwingli, they all on occasion express a

7. Paul Lehmann, *Ethics in a Christian Context* (New York: Harper & Row, 1963),
p. 148.

8. Stanley Hauerwas, "Natural Law, Tragedy and Theological Ethics," in *Truthful-
ness and Tragedy* (Notre Dame: University of Notre Dame Press, 1977), p. 58.

quite ungrudging respect for the moral law naturally implanted in the human heart and seek to inculcate this attitude in their readers. Natural law is not one of the issues on which they bring the Scholastics under criticism. With safeguards of their primary doctrines, but without conscious resistance on their part, natural law enters into the framework of their thought and is an assumption of their political and social teaching. . . . For the Reformers, as for the Fathers, canonists, and Scholastics, natural law stood affirmed on the pages of Scripture.[9]

The pressure to abandon the teaching of natural law stemmed not so much from the Reformation as from post-Enlightenment developments in philosophy, especially utilitarianism and positivism. There was a loss of belief not only in a special divine revelation through Scripture and the church but also in the ability of reason to discern a natural moral order in human affairs. The way was prepared for law to become an instrument of power: might makes right. The positivistic attitude toward law and its validity rendered people impotent in the face of the lawlessness of law. The totalitarian state could successfully manipulate law as a mere function of absolute power. Thus there was no other criterion of validity for the law than the will of those who had the monopoly of force. The twentieth century has paid a heavy price in legalized atrocities and crimes against humanity as a result of the ascendancy of legal positivism in classrooms, legislatures, and courtrooms. After World War II, it seemed as though many people had had enough. Protestant theologians were invited to reconsider the relation between Christian faith and law. Churches gained a renewed sense of responsibility for the process and quality of law in social life. The World Council of Churches and the Lutheran World Federation sponsored conferences to discuss the proper theological response to legal positivism. They debated whether Christian ethics and natural law are in fact antithetical or perhaps instead complementary.

The results of the conferences and new publications in the field of Christian ethics showed that Protestant theologians were in a quandary about natural law. Theologians such as Helmut Thielicke[10] and Walter

9. John T. McNeill, "Natural Law in the Teaching of the Reformers," *Journal of Religion* 26 (1946): 168.

10. Helmut Thielicke, *Theological Ethics* (Philadelphia: Fortress Press, 1966), pp. 383-454.

Künneth[11] moved away from Barth's rejection of natural law, but were still concerned to reiterate the chief Protestant theological objections to the concept. Natural law came to be seen as a kind of necessary evil, or as an illegitimate child who could not be completely abandoned, but whose rights must be severely restricted.

The chief reason why these theologians hesitated to give much playing time to natural law was their awareness of the power of sin. Natural law seems to suggest that the order of being in the original creation has not been totally disrupted by the fall and sin. And it suggests further that human reason is not so blinded as to be incapable of reading the will of God in the natural structures of creation. For these theologians, on the contrary, the *imago Dei* is so fully destroyed that there remains only a negative relationship to God. Natural law theory is guilty of elevating reason above revelation as the criterion and standard of what is right and wrong, true and false. In a fallen world, there are no absolute laws or immutable orders untainted by sin. Thielicke says that, since the fall, we confront at best "orders of preservation." And Künneth speaks of "emergency orders" through which God is working to sustain human life in a fallen world. Natural law also lacks the eschatological perspective that relegates all orders of life to provisional status, always ambiguous and incomplete, moving along in history in the realm of contingency and novelty.

Despite their criticisms, theologians such as Thielicke and Künneth cannot really dispense with natural law. They recognize that it has abiding significance as the sign of the human quest for justice and right. Heuristically, it functions as a goad to the pursuit of approximate justice in an imperfect world. The church needs to respect the common search for justice and law and to promote cooperation between Christians and non-Christians in all spheres of public life. Nonetheless, even with such halfhearted concessions to natural law, it seems clear that these Protestant theologians could not make significant contributions to its renewal and furtherance in society. They write of it with an uneasy conscience, as though natural law has become forbidden fruit for Protestant theology.

Catholic theologians rightly complain that, when Protestants write about natural law, they always take the worst-case scenario, as though

11. Walter Künneth, *Politik Zwischen Dämon und Gott; eine christliche Ethik des Politischen* (Berlin: Lutherisches Verlagshaus, 1954).

there has not also been a history of revision of natural law theory.[12] They complain that, when Protestant theologians write about natural law, they see it as something fixed, always and everywhere the same and always perceptible as such, as though it existed above and beyond history in a static world of eternal principles. Caricatures of natural law abound in Protestant textbooks on social and political ethics. We have only to cite the works of Jacques Maritain and John Courtney Murray to see that the usual caricatures do not match the actual representations of natural law theory under the conditions of modern times.[13] Who would wish to argue that these Catholic intellectuals are out of touch with the changing and diverse constellation of factors that the facts of historical development impose on the church and its social context? Their commitment to natural law did not make them medieval philosophers who would depreciate historical particularity and historical process or ignore the imperative that the concrete uniqueness of each situation of decision and action be attended to. On the other hand, the common criticism of Roman Catholic natural law theorists on the part of Protestant theology is twofold: as Catholics, in distinction from the Protestant Reformers, they do not take sin seriously; as Romans, they are bound to a medieval philosophy — namely, Aristotelian Thomism — and thus cannot take history seriously. Such caricatures and charges are the stuff of which serious ecumenical conversations could be made. But as far as I know, that is a task that remains to be accomplished.

An ecumenical dialogue on the place of natural law in Christian social ethics is particularly necessary and timely, in my opinion, as a kind of counterattack against the wholesale deconstruction of the classical moral and legal principles on which Western culture is founded. Deconstructionism and its academic allies hold that meaning and truth are imposed on texts and situations and are not inherent in the way things are created. The pursuit of truth and justice is increasingly spurned in the academy and replaced with "politically correct ideology." Moral relativism joins with political activism to sabotage the rules and

---

12. Cf. Theodor Her, *Zur Frage nach dem Naturrecht im deutschen Protestantismus der Gegenwart* (München: Verlag Ferdinand Schoningh, 1972); Wilhelm Steinmüller, *Evangelische Rechtstheologie*, 2 vols. (Köln: Bohlau Verlag, 1968).

13. Cf. Michael Novak, "The Achievement of Jacques Maritain," *First Things* 8 (December 1990): 39-44; and Dennis P. McCann, "Natural Law, Public Theology and the Legacy of John Courtney Murray," *The Christian Century*, 5-12 September 1990, p. 801.

50   CARL E. BRAATEN

standards needed to implement a societal system ordered by principles of justice and truth. When the normlessness and the nihilistic effects of the deconstructionist mindset are no longer confined to academia but invade the wider public, the way is prepared for the moral collapse of social institutions or for the enthronement of the totalitarian state. The love affair of some of the founding deconstructionists with the Nazis has been widely reported and has not been refuted by their disciples.[14] Perhaps it is time to expose the relativist and nihilist theories as the underside of totalitarian ideologies and political authoritarianism. Some might object that our call to revive interest in natural law is pointless, like rearranging the deck chairs on the Titanic. The role of Christians is, rather, to be with the chaplains consoling the passengers on their way down, or to abandon ship and look for a lifesaver.

A Critical Correlation of Biblical Revelation and Natural Law

As we have indicated, there was in early dialectical theology an extreme antithesis between biblical revelation and natural law. Those following Barth felt that they had to say an absolute no to reason. There followed, in the name of faithfulness to biblical revelation, a kind of contempt for natural theology, natural law, and natural reason. After that, as we saw, some Protestants allowed a limited role for natural law in the construction of social ethics, but mostly as a symbolic sign of the human quest for justice in the social order.

Natural law is the only available basis of morality for non-Christians, people who do not live within the covenant community and do not share its history and memories. At the same time, there are Protestant theologians who hold to a positive correlation, correspondence, and cooperation between revelation and natural law. In their view there is no necessary opposition between evangelical faith that focuses on the justification of the ungodly on account of Christ and the Catholic doctrine of natural law with its appeal to a universal justice and morality to which people have access through their reason and conscience. An eclectic variety of Protestants holds to a more positive view of natural law, from a Lutheran such as Paul Althaus to a Reformed theologian such as Emil Brunner and to a

14. Cf. Dinesh D'Souza, "Illiberal Education," *The Atlantic Monthly*, March 1991, pp. 51-79.

philosophical theologian such as Paul Tillich. Wolfhart Pannenberg also comes down decidedly on the side of finding an anthropological foundation for asserting a common core of justice and law to which all people in principle have access through reason and conscience, although the particulars of that common ground are provisional, relative, and always ambiguous under the conditions of our finite human existence. Pannenberg keeps the eschatological horizon in focus at all times.

The correlation approach that is open to a new affirmation of natural law would also seek a rehabilitation of reason. Reason has suffered a tragic history, and often Protestants have derived a certain *Schadenfreude* from every report of its demise. If and when reason is discredited, suffers calamity and chaos, theology seems to be justified in making a retreat to the safe haven of fideism. With reason disqualified, faith becomes overloaded and the wires of faith overheated, and direct sorties of faith into the public realm must be expected, without benefit of any rational accountability. We may call this the Ayatollah Khomeini phenomenon in the political realm, and it is equally dangerous no matter in whose God's name the crusade is being undertaken.

It is necessary to correct the widespread assumption that there can be no access to natural law from the presuppositions of Reformation theology, as though its view of Scripture, revelation, Christ, salvation, and faith barred the door to every kind of natural theology, natural law, and rational morality. But it must be equally clear that evangelical theology will hold to a highly circumscribed view of natural law, one that is placed within theological brackets, so that it does not function in separation from the whole of theology.

Edmund Schlink, former professor of systematic and ecumenical theology at Heidelberg University, spelled out the conditions under which a theologian can take up natural law. Natural law cannot be a doctrine that establishes the rights of humankind before God. Humans have no rights *coram Deo*, but only *coram hominibus*. Because of the fall into a sinful situation, there is no ontological continuity between the original creation and the new creation that is apprehended through faith alone. The church's primary task is to proclaim Christ to the nations for the world's salvation.[15]

15. Evangelical catholics in the Lutheran tradition can only applaud Pope John Paul II's most recent encyclical, *Redemptoris Missio*, which clearly sounds the clarion call for the resumption of Christian mission in all parts of the world and criticizes the kind of missiology that teaches that all religions are equally true and salvific.

Nevertheless, the church does have a political responsibility during the interim between the first and the final advent of Christ. It is within this interim that the limited but necessary function of natural law must be maintained.

Lutherans need not have any confessional scruples about affirming such a limited role for natural law. It is necessary to observe the proper distinction between the *coram* relationships. *Coram Deo* and *coram hominibus* are two different levels of relationship. *Coram Deo,* humans are not capable of doing anything that is right before God, anything on the basis of which God is required to set humans in a right relationship with himself. Sin disrupts the right relationship between God and humanity. But this does not negate the fact that humans are capable of doing what is good and right in the order of human relationships, *coram hominibus.* Natural law possesses no theological significance in the sense of providing a basis for human salvation. This soteriological proviso will always make it appear that natural law barely limps along in Reformation theology. However, the negative verdict on natural law in the vertical dimension *coram Deo* need not entail a corresponding rejection of natural law on the horizontal line *coram hominibus* and *coram mundo.* The choice between biblical revelation and natural law is a false one.

A concept of natural law in critical correlation with evangelical theology need not retain the particular metaphysical foundations it received in the medieval Thomistic-Aristotelian synthesis. The idea of a law rooted in the nature of humanity and the world and discoverable by reason has been traced back to the "dawn of conscience."[16] The history of natural law shows a wide variety of interpretations and applications. The Protestant polemic against natural law has been directed primarily against the medieval Thomistic theory of natural law, but that does not mean that the Protestant mind must be closed to any and every concept of natural law. The word "nature" in natural law can mean different things. It may mean the immanent structure of human reason, that which all human beings have in common by virtue of being human beings. Its theological correlate would thus simply be the *imago Dei.* Or "nature" may refer to an ideal state in some Golden Age in the past, as in Rousseau's "return to nature," uncorrupted by civilization. Or it may refer to the fallen condition of humanity, as in the familiar words of

16. Cf. James Luther Adams, "The Law of Nature: Some General Considerations," *The Journal of Religion* 25 (1945): 88.

the confession: "We confess unto thee, O Lord, that we are by nature sinful and unclean."

There are similar variations of meaning with respect to the term "law." "Law" may refer to a moral principle written into human hearts by God and therefore possessing universal validity. Or law may be something imposed on human beings from the outside, by the authority of God or the State or some other power. It may refer to the Ten Commandments, the Torah, or the Sermon on the Mount. It may refer to the inalienable rights of human beings, which all nations are morally bound to acknowledge. When we put "nature" and "law" together, therefore, we confront a legion of possible meanings. We cannot *a priori* foreclose the possibility that a concept of natural law is fully compatible with the framework of a theology faithful to the confessional writings of the Reformation. Thus we cannot agree with Jacques Ellul when he writes: "the doctrine of natural law as a Christian doctrine is thus ruled out at every point."[17]

Principles that Promote a Reinterpretation of Natural Law

I intend now to place natural law within theological brackets determined by basic principles of evangelical catholic theology.

1. We have to begin with the fact that none of the confessional documents of the Reformation, neither those of the Lutheran nor those of the Calvinist traditions, rejected the notion of natural law. There was nothing in their interpretation of the Scriptures that called for such a rejection. In fact, they acknowledged that Scripture teaches that the Gentiles, although outside the scope of God's special revelation to Israel, are able to know something of God's law through the works of creation by means of conscience and reason.[18] To be sure, the Reformers, as biblical theologians, were primarily concerned to draw the proper contrast between the old law and the new on account of Christ. But at the same time they acknowledged that the biblical authors do to some degree recognize elements of the law of God among the Gentiles, a law that in some way must be related to the law of creation that reaches its perfection in Christ.

17. Ellul, *The Theological Foundations of Law*, p. 68.
18. Cf. C. H. Dodd, "Natural Law in the Bible," *Theology*, May/June 1946.

2. An evangelical theology will interpret the role of natural law in light of the hermeneutical distinction between law and gospel. In light of this dialectic between law and gospel, it is possible to develop a Christian understanding of the world and all secular institutions. The word "gospel" refers to the absolute particularity and uniqueness of the message concerning God's coming into the world in the person of Jesus Christ. This places all law in a new light; the legalistic character of the law is contrasted with the creative freedom of the gospel.

3. Along with the particularity of the gospel, which rests on the *solus Christus*, evangelical theology will want to insist on the other *solas*, such as *sola gratia, sola fide*, and *sola scriptura*. But evangelical theology will assert that these *solas* are also good Catholic theology, as Karl Rahner has vigorously argued in *Foundations of Christian Faith*. He writes:

> For a Catholic understanding of the faith there is no reason why the basic concern of Evangelical Christianity as it comes to expression in the three "only's" should have no place in the Catholic Church. Accepted as basic and ultimate formulas of Christianity, they do not have to lead a person out of the Catholic Church. . . . They can call the attention of the Catholic Church again and again to the fact that grace alone and faith alone really are what saves, and that with all our maneuvering through the history of dogma and the teaching office, we Catholic Christians must find our way back to the sources again and again, back to the primary origins of Holy Scripture and all the more so of the Holy Spirit.[19]

With such clear provisos, much of the passionate criticism on the part of Protestant theology directed against the place of natural law in Catholic moral theology might be deflected. The Reformation *solas* function to relativize natural theology, natural law, and the orders of creation theology so that they cannot be used as an independent starting point and approach to the knowledge of God with any salvific potential. The law is not a way of salvation; at best, it is a way in which God's preserving grace is effective in ordering the world.

4. The doctrine of original sin must be taken seriously. This means that the fundamental structure of reality, including the rational and

---

19. Karl Rahner, *Foundations of Christian Faith,* trans. William V. Dych (New York: Seabury Press, 1978), pp. 365, 367.

social nature of humanity, is deeply affected by sin. We live in a fallen world in which demonic forces have been let loose, distorting everything, including human reason. The image of God in humanity is not totally destroyed; rather, it is disoriented, putting humanity in a wrong relationship with God and the world. If the original creation, including the *imago Dei,* is thought to be totally destroyed or depraved, this leads to a kind of Protestant pessimism that places all ethics within the order of redemption and the new creation. This partly accounts for the fact that Protestant ethics has tended to be purely personalistic and voluntaristic, relying on discrete commands announced by God now and then, in this situation or that. Protestant ethics shows a marked tendency to fall into pure occasionalism, actualism, and situationism. The fundamental givens are either denied altogether or ignored, so that the ethical decision is made existentially in each moment and each situation. With the loss of general rules and enduring principles, it is difficult to find a bridge to the public orders of life in which Christians and non-Christians can work side by side.

5. Social ethics will integrate the eschatological perspective into its ethical theory. The eschatological kingdom of God's love is communicated through the gospel as the justification of the ungodly and sinners on account of Christ, but it is communicated through worldly structures of power and justice under the conditions of a sinful world. This is the basis of Luther's distinction between the two realms or two kingdoms, and it correlates with the two states of believing existence in the world, as *simul justus et peccator.*

6. The proper work of love is expressed by the gospel as the forgiveness of sins and new life in Christ. The strange work of love *(opus alienum)* is expressed by the law as God's instrument to effect justice in a world that does not believe in the gospel. Justice is too important a matter for God simply to leave to loving persons. Justice can be accomplished in the world in either of two ways: by the miraculous presence and spontaneity of love or by the pressure and threats of the law. The concept of natural law in one sense is misleading because, when people do what comes naturally, it is neither very just nor very loving. Nevertheless, the idea of natural law is indispensable because it aims to establish a criterion of justice that transcends human conventions or habits and that in some way is universally intelligible. The love of God is strangely at work behind the back of every human being, seeking justice through a law that cannot be identified with mere custom, arbitrariness, power, or interest.

7. Love that expresses itself as justice and by means of law is not at all antithetical to principles and rules that can be clearly formulated to prescribe as well as to guide the ethical decisions and moral actions of human beings and institutions. The antinomian idea that love cannot be mediated by rule and principle has sneaked into situation ethics and hides behind the *agape* label, as though there were no way to translate love into the language of moral norms and principles.

8. When the rule of God's love expresses itself indirectly and *sub contrario* through structures of justice and law, rules can be formulated in advance of particular situations. For example, rules with respect to freedom and equality have been formulated in the United Nations Declaration of Human Rights. Similarly, there could be no World Court to try war criminals if there were no preexisting consensus on what is lawful in warfare. The notion that there are no rules but only situations is an unrealistic appraisal of the human condition outside of Paradise, this side of Eden. Thus the primary commitment of Christian ethics to the truth and power of love, as manifest supremely in the Christ event, relates to law in a dialectically differentiated way, true to the complexities of the human situation within the fallen world and the new things inaugurated by the inbreaking of God's kingdom in Jesus Christ.

9. Social ethics will necessarily correlate eschatology and natural law, or it will forfeit its right to be considered a biblically Christian viewpoint. One chief problem of traditional natural law theory is that it seems to be more at home in a deistic view of God and the world than in a trinitarian vision, which alone can span the whole field of reality from creation to consummation. The final truth of all things is revealed by the arrival of the eschatological future in the person of Jesus Christ. The eschatological future of the kingdom is the power that draws all people, whether they know it or not. This power has been revealed in Jesus Christ as the highest good, which all people implicitly seek in their quest for fulfillment. Therefore, when people strive for justice under the conditions of its absence — and this goes on in all societies — they are in quest of something true and transcendent that for them is still future and yet to be fulfilled. From the Christian point of view, this highest good is the kingdom of God, which Jesus proclaimed and embodied in his very person. The universal human quest for justice can be seen to be the anticipatory presence of the kingdom of God at work throughout the created order, even under the conditions of sin and

estrangement. Natural law can be viewed as the presence of the kingdom of God in the universal human striving for what is good and right. It is fortunate that "natural law" has been kept alive in Roman Catholic moral theology, but it is somewhat regrettable that often it has survived in a noneschatological framework and therefore is often also not attuned to the dynamics of history. The merits of the natural law tradition must be taken up into the framework of an eschatological perspective.

10. Openness to the tradition of natural law prevents Christian ethics from absorbing itself totally within the realm of individual personal relationships, which has been the trend in Protestant existentialism. While it is necessary to distinguish between the individual-personal and the social-political dimensions of the kingdom of God, it is important not to separate them as though the realm of personal relations were unrelated to the realm of social involvements and political institutions. The non-eschatological form of the two-kingdoms ethic in conservative Lutheranism has tended to dichotomize personal ethics and social ethics.

11. When natural law is baptized by Christian theology, it may be seen as the means by which God is ordering the world on its way forward to the final judgment and consummation. The hope of the world does not lie in optimism about nature and law. The mission of the church does not lie in teaching the world about natural law and administering its institutions according to principles of justice and law. The church's true mission does not lie in patching up the old creation but in announcing and celebrating the advent of a new creation in Christ. Even the most splendidly ordered world, even a veritable utopia on earth, would still exist in open rebellion against the gospel, counting on a righteousness of works in opposition to the righteousness of unmerited grace that is a gift from above.

12. The introduction of the eschatological perspective may be disheartening to Christians who dream about a Christian world order and rely on Christian social activism to save the world, or who believe the church ought to remake the world after its own image. On the other hand, the strategy of linking the eschatological perspective to natural law to provide common ground for Christians and non-Christians to share burdens for maintaining and ordering the world may appear as compromise to radical Christians who hear the call of the gospel to leave the world and escape the coming fire and judgment. However, for Christians who take the intermediate position and accept responsi-

bility for the preservation and ordering of the world, this baptized form of natural law will be of real use. We may think of this in terms of believers cooperating with God in preserving the world so that the world may be given time to learn of its true destiny in the kingdom of God.

13. It may appear that the eschatological perspective has so relativized natural law that it hardly deserves to be called natural law anymore. In that perspective, our liberties are relative, our rights are relative. There are no absolute laws, no unconditioned principles in this world, which, from the perspective of God's judgment, is passing away and is meanwhile maintained only by permission of the divine patience. We have set limits to natural law by placing it within theological brackets because from the perspective of God's final revelation in Jesus Christ not too much should be expected from the possibilities of human nature and human reason. God does not save the world through natural law; God does not reconcile the world through the pursuit of justice; God does not transform human hearts through the struggles for human rights; God does not create a community of love by all of our best efforts to order the world for the better. To know this is to draw the proper distinction between law and gospel, as Lutherans would put it, or between nature and grace, as Catholics have traditionally said it. There is a distinction between these different conceptualities, but not of the kind or to a degree that would necessitate Protestants' continued rejection of natural law for the sake of magnifying the gospel.

The Church's Political Hopes for the World; or, Diognetus Revisited

GEORGE WEIGEL

In the summer of 1994 I was invited to address a retreat attended by most of the Roman Catholic bishops of the United States. The retreat's theme — a grating testimony to the modern ecclesiastical bureaucracy's participial addiction — was "Shepherding a Future of Hope." And my assigned topic was "Hope in Society."

I think at least some of the Lords Spiritual were expecting a bit of "social justice" shoptalk, perhaps spiced by a few lurid details about the partisan wars in the Potomac fever swamps, where I have my office. But I began then, and I begin now in discussing "the church's political hopes for the world," not with our late twentieth century, or with the impending twenty-first century, but with the second century, the time of "the churches the apostles left behind."[1] My text is the *Epistula ad Diognetum*, the *Letter to Diognetus*, which has become an important patristic reference point for contemporary Roman Catholic social thought.[2]

---

1. The phrase, though not the time frame, is from Raymond E. Brown, *The Churches the Apostles Left Behind* (New York: Paulist Press, 1984).

2. For the text of *Diognetus*, see *The Apostolic Fathers*, 2nd ed., trans. J. B. Lightfoot and J. R. Hammer, edited and revised by Michael W. Holmes (Grand Rapids: Baker, 1989), pp. 296-306. To provide patristic warrant for their teaching that "each individual layman must be a witness before the world to the resurrection and life of the Lord Jesus, and a sign of the living God" (*Lumen Gentium*, 38), the Fathers of the Second Vatican Council cited *Diognetus* 6.1. The *Letter to Diognetus* is also referenced three times in the new *Catechism of the Catholic Church:* on the duties of Christian citizens (2240); on the right to life of the unborn (2271); and on the "public" meaning of the Lord's Prayer as directed to the One who is "in heaven" (2796).

Resident Aliens

We don't know who Diognetus was; nor do we know who wrote him a letter. But that anonymous Christian apologist created an image of the church-in-the-world that has had a powerful influence on Christian reflection ever since, when he suggested that "What the soul is to the body, Christians are to the world."[3]

To be the *soul* of the world: the image carries with it dialectical or paradoxical connotations of distance and intimacy, the present and the future, the mundane and the transcendent. Those implications are further spelled out when the *Letter to Diognetus* describes Christians-in-the-world in these terms:

> Christians are not distinguished from the rest of humanity by country, language, or custom. For nowhere do they live in cities of their own, nor do they speak some unusual dialect, nor do they practice an eccentric life-style. . . . But while they live in both Greek and barbarian cities, as each one's lot was cast, and follow the local customs in dress and food and other aspects of life, at the same time they demonstrate the remarkable and admittedly unusual character of their own citizenship. They live in their own countries, but only as aliens; they participate in everything as citizens, and endure everything as foreigners. Every foreign country is their fatherland, and every fatherland is foreign. They marry like everyone else, and have children, but they do not expose their offspring. They share their food but not their wives. They are "in the flesh," but they do not live "according to the flesh." They live on earth but their citizenship is in heaven. They obey the established laws; indeed in their private lives they transcend the laws.[4]

3. *Letter to Diognetus* 6.1.
4. *Letter to Diognetus* 5.1-10. The author of *Diognetus* goes on to make clear that the "unusual character" of their citizenship had some unusual consequences for Christians:

> They love everyone and by everyone they are persecuted. They are unknown, yet they are condemned; they are put to death, yet they are brought to life. They are poor, yet they make many rich; they are in need of everything, yet they abound in everything. They are dishonored, yet they are glorified in their dishonor; they are slandered, yet they are vindicated. They are cursed, yet they bless; they are insulted, yet they offer respect. When they do good, they are punished as evildoers; when they are punished, they rejoice as though brought to life. . . . Those who hate them are unable to give a reason for their hostility.

This image of the "resident alien" nicely captures the worldly position of Christians, which is distinctive because it is always in the manner of an experiment. There is one Christian orthodoxy; but there is no single mode of Christian being-in-the-world. Sometimes the Christian in the world will be more comfortably "resident"; at other times, the wickedness of the principalities and powers will require us to be more defiantly "alien," even "sectarian" (which can be a synonym for "faithful"). At all times, though, Christians live "in the world" in a somewhat unsettled condition. For "the world," in Christian perspective, is both the arena of God's action in history *and* an antechamber to our true Home, which is "the city of the living God" (Heb. 12:22).

Through the "resident alien" image, *Diognetus* also reminds us that the most important thing Christians say about the world and its politics — indeed, the most important thing Christians say about *all* of life — is that "Jesus Christ is Lord" (Phil. 2:11). That brief christological confession is the only true source of, and the only secure ground for, our hope. Anything else is simply optimism. And while optimism can be a fragile commodity in the world of politics, Christian hope, built on the transformative conviction that Jesus is Lord, is the sturdy, enduring theological virtue that "responds to the aspiration to happiness which God has placed in the heart of every man" — an aspiration Christians pursue by "placing our trust in Christ's promises and relying not on our own strength, but on the help of the grace of the Holy Spirit."[5]

Ahead of Time

Lived out in "the world" and amid the agitations of the politics of the world, Christian hope should reflect the temporal paradox of Christian life — namely, that Christians are a people ahead of time. Christians are the people who know, and who ought to live as if they knew, that the Lord of history is, in the final analysis, in charge of history. Christians are the people who know how the story is going to turn out; and that puts Christians in a unique position vis-à-vis the flow of history. As Hans Urs von Balthasar has put it, Christians are the ones who,

5. *Catechism of the Catholic Church*, 1818, 1817.

amid the world's accelerating development, "can confront [that evolution] with a divine plan of salvation that is coextensive with it, indeed that always runs ahead of it because it is eschatological."[6]

Christians know how the story is going to turn out. And it is in this sense of "making sense" of the world that the *Letter to Diognetus* can claim that, while "Christians are detained in the world as if in a prison, they in fact hold the world together."[7] Christians know and bear witness to the fact that, in the power of the Spirit, God and his Christ will be vindicated. Or, to recall a phrase that caused a stir a few years ago, Christians know all about "the end of history."[8] Christians know that, at the end of history, the world's story, which is anticipated in the church's story, will be consummated in the Supper of the Lamb, in the New Jerusalem in which "night shall be no more." Christians know that the world's story will be fulfilled beyond the world, in that true City where the elect shall "need no light of lamp or sun, for the Lord God will be their light, and they shall reign for ever and ever" (Rev. 22:5).

Now if *that* is what you know — if *that* is the conviction on which your life is built, and if *that* is the perception that orients your apprehension of reality — well, that gives you a rather distinctive "take" on the world and its politics. The further paradox is that it is precisely the *eschatological* dimension of Christian hope that creates the moral and cultural conditions in which it is possible to build a pluralist democracy whose public life contributes to genuine human flourishing. But that is to get ahead of ourselves. For the moment, the crucial thing to grasp is that, as the church, our hope as lived in "the world" cannot be anything other than a reflection of our conviction that the end of the story — the end of our story, and the end of the world's story — has already been disclosed in the resurrection of Jesus Christ and his ascension to the right hand of the Father in glory.

6. Hans Urs von Balthasar, "Church and World," in *Truth Is Symphonic: Aspects of Christian Pluralism* (San Francisco: Ignatius Press, 1987), p. 98.

7. *Letter to Diognetus* 6.7.

8. See Francis Fukuyama, "The End of History?" *The National Interest* 16 (Summer 1989): 1-18.

Eschatological Hope and Worldly Courage

Formed by that truth (which is the central truth of history), and within those aforementioned dialectics of intimacy and distance, present and future, the mundane and the transcendent, Christian "resident aliens" can tackle their tasks as citizens without kicking against the goads in a frantic attempt to "force" the Kingdom into history here and now.[9] A popular contemporary Roman Catholic hymn bids us to "build the City of God." I'm sorry, but I must decline. Christians who think themselves obliged to "build the City of God" suffer from a theological misapprehension whose political consequences, history has taught us, can run from the picaresque through the foolish and on to the grotesque.

No; that fevered urgency for a political construction of the Kingdom is not the way Christians ought to think of their worldly obligations. Knowing that the Son, the first-born of many brethren (Rom. 8:29), has been raised to glory, and knowing that he, not we, will build the City of God, we can relax a bit about the world and its politics — not to the point of indifference or insouciance or irresponsibility, but in the firm conviction that, in the extremity of the world's agony and at the summit of its glories, Jesus remains Lord. And our primary responsibility, as Christian disciples, is to remain faithful to the bold proclamation of *that* great truth. For *that* is the truth the world most urgently needs to hear — 2,000 years ago, today, and until God's Kingdom comes, in God's time and by God's gracious initiative.

Moreover, it is in the pondering of that salvific truth that we discover the courage to live out the "hope that is within" us (1 Peter 3:15). The world, to put it bluntly, can be a pain in the neck — and the politics of the world, even more so. The frenzied "politics of the Kingdom" is not the only temptation set before Christians-in-the-world. The temptation to an eschatological indifference is also perennial, as is the temptation to cynicism, not least along the Potomac littoral where I live. From where, then, do we draw the courage to engage the world and its politics, and in a manner befitting those

9. A temptation that goes back, on some readings of the New Testament evidence, to the original apostolic band. See, for example, Dorothy L. Sayers's reading of Judas in *The Man Born to Be King* (San Francisco: Ignatius Press, 1990).

"born again of water and the Spirit" (John 3:5)? Balthasar finds the source of what he calls "the courage to pursue the path of history"[10] in John 1:14:

> Only Christianity has the courage to affirm the present, because God has affirmed it. He became a man like ourselves. He lived in our alienation and died in our God-forsakenness. He imparted the "fullness of grace and truth" (John 1.17) to our here and now. He filled our present with his presence. But since the divine presence embraces all "past" and all "future" in itself, he has opened up to us all the dimensions of time. The Word that became flesh is the "Word in the beginning"; in him we have been "chosen before the foundation of the world." It is also the "final word," in which everything in heaven and on earth shall be caught up together: Alpha and Omega. . . . [Thus] it is not possession, but a being-possessed, that lends wings to Christian hope. It vibrates with the thought that the earth should reply to heaven in the way that heaven has addressed earth. It is not in his own strength that the Christian wants to change the earth, but with the power of grace of him who — transforming all things — committed his whole self for him.[11]

Because the world was formed by the Word, the world, even in the grasp of sin, has an innate intelligibility; "the world" is not the arena of absurdity or madness. Because the world has been *trans*formed by the incarnate Word who *dwelt among us,* the Christian disciple cannot despise or despair of the world. For the world has been impressed with "a new spiritual form, chiselled on the very stone of existence": the form of the Incarnate and Crucified One who is also and forever the Risen One.[12] The worldly vocation of a Christian can take the form of a contemplative withdrawal from "the world," in which the contemplative dies to worldly things precisely as a sacrificial offering for the salvation of the world. But for most Christians, the obligation to engage the world in which the Word dwelt, "full of grace and truth" (John 1:17), will be fulfilled in the form of action informed by contemplative reflec-

10. See Balthasar, "Church and World," p. 98.
11. Hans Urs von Balthasar, "The Three Forms of Hope," in *Truth Is Symphonic,* pp. 190-92.
12. Hans Urs von Balthasar, *The Glory of the Lord: A Theological Aesthetics,* vol. 1: *Seeing the Form* (San Francisco: Ignatius Press, 1982), p. 36.

tion.[13] And so we come to the question of "the church's political hope for the world."

The Public Difference the Church Makes

"The church's political hope for the world." Put another way, what does that church ask of the world? And does that asking suggest certain hopes — or, perhaps better, prudential judgments — about the right ordering of that part of the world that is the πολις: the political community, the society organized politically for common, purposeful action?

Here, it might seem, is where we discover the "church's agenda for the world." But there is no such agenda. Or at least there is no agenda such as that suggested by Christian Coalition congressional scorecards, U.S. Catholic Conference voter guides, "JustLife" candidate evaluation criteria, or the sundry public policy pronouncements of the main-line/oldline justice-and-peace curias. These artifacts may be interesting or boring, enlightening or obfuscating, wise or stupid. But they are not, in the strict sense of the term, *ecclesial* statements. They may be statements *from* the church, or from some faction *within* the church; but they are not statements *of* the church. The church is not one political possibility, one political ideology, among many thousands of such possible contestants in the public arena.[14] If the church is to become, in her presentation of herself to "the world," what she "already is and is to be, namely, the leaven that facilitates the ultimate unification of the world in its totality, the enzyme and organism of the eschatological salvation that has appeared in Christ"[15] — if, in other words, the church is to be faithful to her origin in Christ, in the blood and water that flowed from the side of the Crucified One (John 19:34) — then the

13. Contemplation and action are thus not antinomies. "Contemplation melds into action, or it is not contemplation," according to Balthasar. (Cited in Edward T. Oakes, *Pattern of Redemption: The Theology of Hans Urs von Balthasar* [New York: Crossroad, 1994], p. 147.)

14. Thus John Paul II, in the 1991 social encyclical *Centesimus Annus*, asserts that the social doctrine of the church "is not an ideology" (46) and has been developed "not in order to recover former privileges or to impose [the church's] own vision" of the right ordering of politics (53), but as an "indispensable and ideal orientation" (43), a horizon of reflection radiating from the "care and responsibility for man" entrusted to the church by Christ (53), and thus constituting a "valid instrument for evangelization" (54).

15. Balthasar, "Church and World," p. 96.

church cannot have an agenda that is commensurable with other "political" agendas.

But that does not mean that the church has nothing to ask of the world. And that asking carries within it certain implications about the right ordering of the political community.

Thus, to the immediate business at hand:

1. The first thing the church asks of the world is the space — social, legal, political, even psychological — in which to carry out her distinctive ministry of word and sacrament.

The church asks the world to let the church be the church. Put more sharply, the church expects and, if circumstances warrant, the church *demands* that she be allowed to be what she is: a reality "in the nature of a sacrament — a sign and instrument . . . of communion with God and unity among all men."[16] The first thing the church asks the world is that she be allowed to be herself.

Now this is, to be sure, no small thing. Nor is it a private matter, so to speak. The first thing the church asks of the world has real-world implications for the world, and especially for that part of the world we call the "state," the juridical embodiment of the political community. For the only kind of state that can grant the first thing the church asks is a state that neither claims nor seeks any final authority over the church's ministry of word and sacrament, which in turn implies a *limited* state, whose powers are circumscribed by custom (i.e., by moral-cultural *habit*) and by law. Thus the first thing the church asks of "the world" is that that part of the world called "the state" adopt for itself a self-limiting ordinance.

The church's first request of the world — that the church might proceed, unimpeded, with its singular mission — implies a deep critique of the totalitarian temptation, in both its hard fascist or communist form and its softer modern bureaucratic forms. The latter is worth dwelling on for just a moment. We all understand that something was fundamentally wrong when Nazi Germany attempted to co-opt the church for political ends or when the Soviet Union under Lenin, Stalin, and their heirs tried to obliterate the church (and to co-opt that which was not obliterated), just as we understand that the persecution of the church in China, Sudan,

---

16. Vatican II, *Lumen Gentium*, 1.

and Saudi Arabia today is an evil that bespeaks a fundamentally disordered political community. But we should also understand that the modern bureaucratic state's temptation to expand the reach of its regulatory power can, even in established democracies, constitute a denial of the first thing that the church asks of the world. When the U.S. Department of Housing and Urban Development "asks" the Roman Catholic Archdiocese of Los Angeles to change the name of a large shelter for the homeless, which is the recipient of modest federal funds, from the "St. Vincent de Paul Shelter" to the "Mr. Vincent de Paul Shelter," something is seriously awry. It is not, to be sure, so desperately awry as the kidnapping of Christian children in the south Sudan and their being sold into slavery. But it is awry nonetheless, and it bespeaks a disinclination on the part of the state to grant the first request the church makes of the world, which implies a disinclination on the part of the state to recognize the limits of its own competence and power. And that is bad news for democracy, as well as for the mission of the church.

By being herself, the church also serves a critical demythologizing function in a democracy. The eschatological character of the church's hope relativizes all worldly expectations and sovereignties; and in doing so, the church's eschatological hope constitutes a barrier against the coercive politics of worldly utopianism. Rousseau had it exactly backwards when he argued that Christian convictions "made any reasonable civil order impossible."[17] The opposite is the case: by locating the finality of our hope (and thus the object of our highest sovereign allegiance) in the time beyond time, the church helps create the space for a free, vigorous, and civil interplay of a variety of proposals for ordering public life, none of which is invested with ultimate authority. Democracy is impossible when politics is absolutized. Thus in this sense Christian eschatology makes democracy and the politics of persuasion possible.

If a *limited* state is one implication of the first thing the church asks of the world, then the second implication is pluralism. Indeed, the two are closely related. For the limited state is a state that recognizes that the political community is not the only community to which human beings owe allegiance.

The church's claim for "free space" for its mission and ministry is one crucial opening to the possibility of a plurality of communities within

17. Cited in Christoph Schönborn, "The Hope of Heaven, the Hope of Earth," *First Things* 52 (April 1995): 32-38.

society, to which men and women are bound with strong ties of commitment and affection. Moreover, the Christian conviction that there need be no essential contradiction (although there will always be tensions) between the obligations of discipleship and the obligations of citizenship in a rightly ordered polity demonstrates that genuine pluralism, far from leading to social chaos, contributes to the public order that every state is obliged to promote. The Christian claim for "free space" is not simply anti-totalitarian in its public implications; more positively, the church is bullish on pluralism. Pluralism is essential for the church; but experience has shown that pluralism is also essential for the political community, or at least for any political community that aspires to freedom. For there can be no freedom without the free mediating institutions of civil society, which are, as Tocqueville recognized, the first "political institutions" of a democracy, precisely because they establish the crucial distinction between society and the state, and society's "priority" over the state (morally and, one might even say, ontologically).[18]

> *2. The second thing the church asks of the world is that the world consider the possibility of its redemption.*

As we know from the martyrologies, the world sometimes does not take kindly to the church's proposal that it consider whether it might be in need of redemption, and whether that redemption might have been effected in Christ. Indeed, this has been an exceptionally costly request in the twentieth century, which is the greatest century of martyrdom in the history of the church — a fact that barely registers on the consciousness of most North American Christians. Yet Pope John Paul II sees in the twentieth-century rebirth of a "church of martyrs" both a preparation for the "springtime of evangelization" that should characterize the twenty-first century and the fulfillment of the church's longing for unity. The "most convincing form of ecumenism," the pope wrote recently, "is the ecumenism of the saints and of the martyrs. The *communio sanctorum* speaks louder than the things that divide us."[19] In

18. On this point, see John Courtney Murray, *We Hold These Truths: Catholic Reflections on the American Proposition* (Garden City: Doubleday Image Books, 1964), p. 43.

19. John Paul II, *Tertio Millennio Adveniente*, 37; on the next century as a "springtime for the Gospel," see *Redemptoris Missio*, 86.

their common loss of life for the cause of Christ, Protestants, Orthodox, Anglicans, and Catholics have achieved a Christian unity that still eludes the church in the world.[20]

All Christians are called to be martyrs — not necessarily to the point of loss of life, but in the original sense of the μαρτυς or "witness."[21] That to which the Christian bears witness is the truth about God and man revealed in the life, death, and resurrection of Jesus Christ. And that is the truth that the church asks the world to consider: Jesus Christ, who "fully reveals man to himself and brings to light his most high calling";[22] Jesus Christ, the "answer to the question that is every human life."[23]

In our own circumstances in late twentieth-century America, the church's proclamation of this truth and the church's invitation to the world to consider the possibility of its redemption meet less with a direct denial by the πολις of the Christian soteriological claim (which would typically result in a direct persecution of the church) than with a kind of indifference to the whole business. God, Christ, redemption, sanctification — surely all of these are beyond the pale for serious, mature, postmodern adults, concerned as they are with authenticity and autonomy. The Christian claim may be a pious myth, capable of producing citizens (especially lower-class citizens) with desirable behavioral characteristics. But that the Christian claim poses *the* issue

---

20. John Paul II developed this point further in his 1995 encyclical on ecumenism, *Ut Unum Sint:*

> In a theocentric vision, we Christians already have a common martyrology. This also includes the martyrs of our own century, more numerous than one might think, and it shows how, at a profound level, God preserves communion among the baptized in the supreme demand of faith, manifested in the sacrifice of life itself. The fact that one can die for the faith shows that other demands of the faith can also be met. I have already remarked, and with deep joy, how an imperfect but real communion is preserved and is growing at many levels of ecclesial life. I now add that this communion is *already* perfect in what we all consider the highest point of the life of grace, *martyria* unto death, the truest communion possible with Christ who shed his blood, and by that sacrifice brings near those who once were far off (cf. Ephesians 2.13). (*Ut Unum Sint*, 84, emphasis added)

21. On martyrdom as the "form" of discipleship, see John Paul II, *Veritatis Splendor*, 90-94.

22. Vatican Council II, *Gaudium et Spes*, 22.

23. John Paul II, Homily at Camden Yards, Baltimore, October 8, 1995.

involved in understanding the truth of the world — well, we have other things to do.

Even worse than indifference is the calculated insouciance toward the Christian proposal that one typically finds among a certain sort of intellectual in affluent societies today. Despite its self-conscious world-liness, this insouciance constitutes a real and present danger to "the world." For its public expression is the decadence of debonair nihilism; and debonair nihilism has awful public consequences, creating as it does a toxic social and cultural environment whose primary victims are not the well-off but those on the margins of society, who have far less room for error in the conduct of their lives. As we have seen in our inner urban communities, the net result of principled hedonism and debonair nihilism among the intellectualoids and the wealthy is a vast breakdown of social order among the poor. And we need not doubt that, if the chaos were to spread beyond the communities to which it is now largely confined, the further result would be a breakdown of democratic order, in a reach for an authoritarian solution to what would have become an intolerable problem.

Thus, in challenging "the world" to remain open to the possibility of its redemption, the church is helping to nurture (and, where neces-sary, to revivify) certain moral understandings about the cultural foun-dations of democracy and the civil liberties we associate with democracy. You cannot have a democracy without a critical mass of democrats — that is, of people who have committed themselves to the ethos of democratic civility. And between the ethos of democratic civility, on the one hand, and the insouciance of debonair nihilism and principled hedonism, on the other, there is a great gulf fixed that no society may cross.

Put another way, a world that has prematurely and peremptorily dismissed the question of its possible redemption is a world that seems unlikely to be able to secure the cultural foundations on which a civil, democratic society can be built or sustained. Perhaps in other times and places this was not so.[24] But today, when the premature closure of the

24. The Deists among the founding fathers were not, for example, overly concerned about the world's redemption. But as the bishops of the United States argued at the Third Plenary Council of Baltimore in 1884, the American founders "built better than they knew." Or, as John Courtney Murray put it three-quarters of a century later, the success of the American democratic experiment rested, not on the thin epistemological and anthropological foundations of "eighteenth-century individualistic rationalism," but

world to the question of its possible redemption is often the result of a deep-rooted epistemological skepticism about any matters of truth and falsehood, we have a situation in which the men and women of "the world" cannot give a persuasive and compelling account of why the democratic regime is morally superior to other arrangements.[25] And the principal challenge to this radical skepticism and its attendant moral confusions (and social pathologies) is the Christian church — or, more precisely, Christian orthodoxy. The Nicene Creed contains no blueprint for conducting the politics of "the world." But the church that can faithfully recite the Nicene Creed and defend its plausibility as the Way Things Are is a church capable of giving a much thicker account of its commitment to the dignity of the human person and to the politics of human freedom than much of what is on offer in academic philosophical circles today.

Eucharistic Church, Public Church

This kind of witness in and for the world requires a particular kind of church. The church capable of proposing to "the world" that it consider the possibility of its redemption in Christ is emphatically not a church conceived in mundane terms as another "voluntary organization" with a political task. Rather, the church that can ask the world to consider itself redeemable (and redeemed) is a church that conceives itself eucharistically as the Body of Christ. And as Christ's Body, such a church would share Christ's destiny, which is not a destiny to power, but rather a destiny in which "being given" means being broken and shared out.[26]

---

on the moral culture of a people who had "learned [their] own personal dignity in the school of Christian faith," whether they recognized that patrimony or not. See Murray, *We Hold These Truths*, pp. 45, 50.

The American democratic experiment, like every democratic experiment, depends for its legitimation on warrants it cannot produce in and of itself. For all the inadequacies of their philosophical position, the founders still knew that they had to give an account of their actions, before "nature's God" and in honor of "a decent respect to the opinions of mankind" (as they put it in the Declaration of Independence). The peculiar danger of our present circumstance is the denial of the very possibility of such warrants and such an account by philosophers and political theorists.

25. On this point, see Richard John Neuhaus, "Can Atheists Be Good Citizens?" *First Things* 15 (August/September 1991): 17-21.

26. See Balthasar, "Church and World," p. 96.

This is, to be sure, a post-Christendom church; but that seems appropriate both in itself and in a post-Christendom world. It is also a church at risk; but that, as Balthasar reminds us, has always been the situation of the church. For in being broken and shared out for "the world"

> [the] Church will suffer the loss of its shape as it undergoes a death, and all the more so, the more purely it lives from its source and is consequently less concerned with preserving its shape. In fact, it will not concern itself with affirming its shape but with promoting the world's salvation; as for the shape in which God will raise it from its death to serve the world afresh, it will entrust [that] to the Holy Spirit.[27]

In this regard, it is worth remembering that the inspired portion of the history of the church (i.e., the book of Acts) ends with the account of a shipwreck — and the consequent furtherance of the church's evangelical mission *ad gentes*.[28] Reflection on that imagery should be reassuring as the church considers how it might today propose to "the world" the possibility of its redemption.

A public church eucharistically conceived also enables us to grasp the fact that the *Letter to Diognetus* was expressing a central truth of the Christian reality, not merely a pious sentiment, when our patristic author affirmed that, for Christians, "every foreign country is their fatherland." That is quite obviously not the case in worldly terms, even for the most astute of what we would now call "inculturators." But it is most certainly true when Christians from another homeland gather with fellow believers in a foreign country around the eucharistic table of the Lord. For the past four years, it has been my privilege to be a faculty member at a seminar on modern Catholic social thought and the democratic prospect, held annually in Poland for students from throughout Central and Eastern Europe. As my experience of these students becomes more extensive, I am more and more impressed by the distinctive perspectives they bring to social and political questions from their different national histories and cultural backgrounds. And yet, as those differences impress themselves on me, I am even more

---

27. Balthasar, "Church and World," p. 96.
28. See Balthasar, "Church and World," p. 96.

struck by our unity around the eucharistic table. The church cannot "give" the unity of an ordered and free political community to "the world" on the basis of its eucharistic *communio;* if such a πολις is possible, it will have to be organized in specifically political terms. But the eucharistic community of those Christians for whom every foreign country is a homeland is a powerful counter-case to the claims of the radical dividers and multiculturalists, for whom *Vive le différence* has become the first principle of anthropology.

The kind of eucharistically centered church that can propose the question of its redemption to "the world" is also a church that challenges implicitly (and, at a secondary level of witness, explicitly) the claims variously advanced by Marxists, deconstructionists, authoritarian Confucians, and activist Muslims that the notion of "universal human rights" is a species of Western cultural imperialism, and that there are no "universal human rights" because there is no universal human nature. This is an important public witness to make today, for if there is no universal human nature and no universal moral law, then there can be no universal conversation about the human future; there can be only a Hobbesian world in which all are at war with all.[29]

From a Christian point of view, the unity of the *humanum* will be fully realized only in the Kingdom of God. And the human unity believers experience in the Body of Christ cannot be "transferred" in one-to-one correspondence to "the world." But the *fact* of our unity in Christ across the barriers of sex, race, ethnicity, and culture is a powerful reminder to a sullen and cynical world that the claims of the radical dividers — who, in their various ways, are all monists, whether monists of a single ideology or monists of radical indifference — are not the only, much less the final, word on the human condition and the human prospect.

The Causes for Which We Must Contend

There is, then, no "Christian agenda" for the politics of "the world." But the church's hope for the world includes a number of causes for which we are bound to contend in the world of politics, because of what

29. See my essay, "Are Human Rights Still Universal?" *Commentary* (February 1995): 41-45.

we believe we know about humankind through the revelation of God in Christ.

The most important of these is *religious freedom*.

Here we return to the first thing the church asks of the world. The church cannot be the church if she attempts to put the coercive power of the state behind her truth claims, or if she acquiesces in the state's assumption of that role. Coerced faith is no faith. Or, as the *Letter to Diognetus* puts it, the God of Christians "saves by persuasion, not compulsion, for compulsion is no attribute of God."[30] The church's defense of religious freedom is thus not a matter of institutional self-interest. Religious freedom is, rather, an acknowledgment in the juridical order of a basic truth about the human person that is essential for the right ordering of society. A state that claims competence in the interior sanctuary where the human person meets God is a state that has refused to adopt the self-limiting ordinance essential to right governance (not to mention democracy). Religious freedom is the first of human rights precisely because it is the juridical acknowledgment (in constitutional and/or positive law) that within every human person is a privileged sanctuary of conviction and conscience where state power may not tread; and that acknowledgment is the beginning of limited government. In defending religious freedom, therefore, the church defends both the truth about man and the conditions for the possibility of civil society.[31]

The second cause for which the church must contend is the cause of *pluralism*. What we call "pluralism" today is really plurality: the sociological fact of difference. Plurality is a given, at least in American society. Plura*lism* is a signal cultural accomplishment, the transformation of difference and division into an ordered conversation about the greatest of all political questions, first identified as such by Aristotle: "How, then, should we live together?" The question has an inescapable moral core, disclosed in the verb "should." And so in the Aristotelian tradition (later adopted in various forms by various Christian political

---

30. *Letter to Diognetus* 7.4. This patristic affirmation finds a contemporary echo in the 1986 "Instruction on Christian Freedom and Liberation" from the Congregation for the Doctrine of the Faith, in which Cardinal Joseph Ratzinger writes that "God wishes to be adored by people who are free" (44). Similarly, in *Redemptoris Missio* John Paul II asserts that "the Church proposes; she imposes nothing" (39).

31. The defense of religious freedom, viewed from this angle, is thus an expression of the church's commitment to what in Roman Catholic terms has come to be understood as the core social-ethical principle of *subsidiarity*.

thinkers), politics is always an extension of ethics. To contend for the creation of a genuine pluralism of participation and engagement is one public face, so to speak, of the church's challenge to the world in the matter of the world's possible redemption. For to build a genuine pluralism means to reject any monism of indifference or insouciance about the moral-cultural health of the public square.[32]

Finally, the church must contend for the possibility of *participation* in public life. Here we return to Christian anthropology. As the *Catechism of the Catholic Church* puts it, "'Participation' is the voluntary and generous engagement of a person in social interchange. It is necessary that all participate, each according to his own position and role, in promoting the common good. This obligation is inherent in the dignity of the human person."[33]

The church's defense of participatory democratic freedoms can be justified in terms of prudential judgment. But the most secure ground for the church's defense of democracy is the church's understanding of the revealed truth about humankind as the *imago Dei:* a *person,* not an autonomous self, with intelligence and free will, and thus capable of reflection and decision. The church does not hold (and most certainly ought not hold) that everyone is obliged to engage in the daily business of politics. But because the church proposes to "the world" a vision of the human person in which the defense of individual liberties is intimately related to the responsibility to promote the common good, the church must contend for the possibility of active political participation by those who discern a vocational obligation to those tasks. In this respect, the church is not simply anti-totalitarian and pro-pluralist; the church is in some sense necessarily "populist."

The Heart of the Matter

This construal of the "public church" will undoubtedly strike some as terribly minimalist, perhaps even irresponsible. What, they will ask, about the environment, or the status of women, or welfare reform, or

32. Thus the church's contesting for genuine pluralism becomes, in these circumstances, an expression of the church's commitment to what in Roman Catholic terms has become known as the core social-ethical principle of *solidarity*.

33. *Catechism of the Catholic Church,* 1913.

parental choice in education, or humanitarian intervention in Bosnia, or a flat tax, or the National Endowment for the Arts, or abortion, or euthanasia? I do not wish to suggest that these are not important issues; they are, and in the case of the life issues, they bear directly on the question of whether the American republic will continue to exist in moral-cultural continuity with its founding. But I do mean to suggest that we damage the integrity of the church and its public witness when we suggest, explicitly or implicitly, that politics, understood as the quest for power in the world, engages Christian *hope,* understood as one of the three theological virtues. I think I can make a persuasive case for my position on any of the issues listed just above; and those positions will be informed by what I understand to be the relevant "middle axioms" of Christian social ethics. But the outcome of these questions — which is to say, the politics of these questions — does not touch, directly, "the hope that is within" me (to return to 1 Peter). If it did, there would be something defective about my hope.

Paradoxically, the church that conceives its public witness in the terms I have suggested is, at the same time, the most "relevant" church imaginable, these days. Political analysts working strictly within the boundaries of the social sciences are now coming to understand the truth of Pope John Paul II's assertion that, in terms of the free society today, the really interesting and urgent questions have to do with culture, not with the structures of politics and economics.[34] Thus the political scientist Francis Fukuyama, who notoriously proposed in 1989 that in democratic capitalism we had reached "the end of history," now argues that neither democratic politics nor the market can properly function absent the tempering and guidance provided by moral habits, or what an older generation would have called "virtues." Democracy and the market, in other words, are not machines that will run of themselves; nor can democracy and the free economy be sustained on the basis of liberal-individualist principles alone. Thus Fukuyama discerns a paradox at the heart of the modern free society:

> If the institutions of democracy and capitalism are to work properly, they must co-exist with certain *premodern cultural habits* that ensure their proper functioning. Law, contract, and economic rationality provide a necessary but not sufficient basis for both the stability and

---

34. See, for example, section 5 of *Centesimus Annus,* "State and Culture."

prosperity of postindustrial societies; they must as well be leavened with reciprocity, moral obligation, duty toward community, and trust, which are based in habit rather than rational calculation. The latter are not anachronisms in a modern society but rather the sine qua non of the latter's success.[35]

A church that recognizes the "priority of culture" in the postmodern circumstances of the free society, and whose social witness addresses that society at the deepest level of its self-understanding (as would be the case on the model suggested above), is thus a church positioned precisely on the cutting edge of the debate over the future of freedom. Far from being hopelessly out of it, a church whose social witness is drawn from the most profound source of the "hope that is within" us may sometimes find itself uncomfortably "relevant."

But that, too, can be one of the costs of discipleship.

35. Francis Fukuyama, *Trust: The Social Virtues and the Creation of Prosperity* (New York: Free Press, 1995), p. 11. For a fuller discussion of this proposal, see my essay, "Life After History," in *Commentary*, October 1995, pp. 34-38.

Whose Crisis of Faith?
Culture, Faith, and the American Academy

ANTHONY UGOLNIK

A recent book by George Marsden has struck a chord in the Christian imagination in America. Its title tells its story: *Soul of the American University: From Protestant Establishment to Established Unbelief.*[1] It is one of very many recent books that have documented an estrangement between Christian and secular America. Yet there is a real irony to the note of apology that invades even the burnished blurb on the inside flap of the jacket to the book. Persistent scholars have documented the struggle of the Christian mind to survive. And survive it does, in colleges and universities that view "the Christian mind" as, at best, a relic of a believing past that can subsist no longer. Yet above a photo of Marsden that leaves him looking rather uncomfortable, the book jacket text solemnly protests that within these pages this author proves "that religious perspectives can provide a legitimate contribution to the highest level of scholarship."

Only in America would an academic press assume that Christian scholarship is an oxymoron. As the Jewish scholars Midge Decter and Gertrude Himmelfarb note, the fact that we now use phrases like "Christian America," or "the Christian mind," or "Christian culture" proves that we ourselves are anxious about our identity. In their youth,

---

1. George Marsden, *Soul of the American University: From Protestant Establishment to Established Unbelief* (Oxford: Oxford University Press, 1994).

Portions of this essay appeared in a review of George Marsden's book *Soul of the American University* for *Academic Questions* (Summer 1995).

protest these Christian-friendly Jewish intellectuals, no one would have imagined an America as other than "Christian." When we turn to an issue like culture — the words we read, the images we see, the imagination in which we are immersed — the anxiety is even greater. "Culture wars" is a term that presupposes casualties. The stakes, then, are very high.

At first glance, the odds are against the Christians. Unlike ancient Byzantium, or medieval Europe, or Florence at the *quattrocento*, patrons have ceased, by and large, to fund culture through the people or institutions that produce it. That is, emperors or churches or even the wealthy rarely endow painters or writers directly. We have evolved a curious system whereby we endow the interpreters of culture rather than its primary agents. Institutions of higher learning absorb the lion's share of our cultural dollars and our cultural attention. As Roger Lundin documents in his brilliant book *The Culture of Interpretation,* we have long empowered in America "the spirit of theory."[2] It is the interpreting critic, and not the imagining artist, who directs the mind toward its culture. Culture critics mimic the scientific method. The interpreter, taking refuge in distance from the object to be interpreted, can hover above it rather than becoming immersed within it; it is a state peculiarly friendly to the distance of agnosticism or atheism.

Only in popular culture does our imagination still surrender to the writer or artist with less self-consciousness. There our distance from belief and the believer is assured by civic convention: separation from church and state means, in effect, the divorce of the public imagination from God. Though academics profess never to watch TV, characters in our sitcoms share much in common with the people in the academies that teach our children: they never go to church and are seldom seen praying. No wonder religious perspectives, whatever they might be, are now confined to so narrow a forum.

As an American academic myself, and an Eastern Orthodox priest who has spent much time in Russia before and after "the change," I am in a peculiar position to understand the twin assumptions of popular culture and the academy. With a tie on my chest rather than the three-barred cross I now wear, I used to apply for grants to study in the old USSR. As I survived interviews with tweeded countrymen and women who probed suspiciously at my proposed studies of reli-

2. Roger Lundin, *The Culture of Interpretation* (Grand Rapids: Eerdmans, 1993).

gious culture in the former Soviet Union, I would marvel at the similarity in perspective between American "Sovietologists," as they used to be called, and the Soviet Council for Antireligious Affairs. One of these American academics, a woman whose zealous exportation of feminism to Russia was often funded by the government, said to me, "Quite frankly, we are concerned that you might be seeking to export a religious agenda."

Only after two years in Russia did I realize what it still shocks me to say openly. My academic interviewers did indeed share real and explicit premises with my future Soviet hosts. Secular education in America is, in my eyes, the last survival of the Soviet ideal. I already knew that my procession of past professors and current academic mentors had a kind of "myopia toward mysticism": like Vernon Parrington, their prime intellectual historian, my professors were aware of, but also angry at, America's early Christian origins. But also like Parrington, their awareness of religion modulated itself to either silence or blindness as we approached modernity. My religion, bound to the Christian Orthodox ghetto, had not yet absorbed the relentless progress of the Protestant mainstream toward 1945. That was the year in which the Harvard Report *General Education in a Free Society* effectively bled intellectual tradition of religious content. "In effect," Marsden archly summarizes, "they were recommending a liberal Protestantism with the Christianity removed."[3]

Had I read that report, then, throughout the 1980s, when I was trying to convince Sovietologists of "Russian Orthodox viability" in a hostile state, I would have saved myself some precious time. I would have known that secular American academics, even less than their Soviet counterparts, could not *administratively* acknowledge the survival of a religious tradition in a postmodern context. I would have done earlier what my fellow Russian Orthodox intellectuals, some of them with fresh prison tattoos, eventually taught me to do: cloak my dialogic faith in the chameleonic energy of Mikhail Bakhtin's theory. (Mikhail Bakhtin was a Soviet scholar of literature. If Bakhtin could attend liturgy, confess to a spiritual father, inspire a party of believing intellectuals through the repressive 1970s, and yet be celebrated at Duke as the Marxist he consistently denied he was, then there could be hope for an Orthodox academic in America who knew his place.)

3. Marsden, *Soul of the American University*, p. 389.

Soviets knew that their System brutally silenced the voice of faith. It was a surprise only to former "Sovietologists" that once the System fell, the voice of a believing if wounded intellect would once more be heard in Russia. Marsden and Stephen Carter, Midge Decter and Roger Lundin, a whole host of scholars now raise the same voice, more politely, among us as well. Culture — yes, Christian culture in modernity — depends on whether or not they can be heard. Astonishingly, intellectuals who shape our American academy still believe and profess that modernity, like a vacuum, has swallowed even faith's echo. The energetic crypto-secularism of the 1960s, which Marsden recalls in Harvey Cox's embrace of *The Secular City,* has been depleted. To my somewhat bitter amusement, Harvey Cox, too, has taken an intellectual pilgrimage to Russia to rediscover the Sacred. (As one of my Russian friends said, with some bitterness, "He is welcome to the blood of our martyrs. After what he has wrought, he needs it as a tonic.")

It is thus a painful exercise for us believers within the academy to realize anew the real depth of our exile. Unlike our cohorts in Eastern Europe, we have seen no vindication. Believing intellectuals in America live in a bell jar, set off from the sacred. The vacuum of theory sucks up mystic imagination. As I discovered when I invited a hot new scholar to speak to my medieval class, students of mystic texts are far more likely to hear of gender and sexuality than they are of the substance of medieval belief. This young woman was to address my class on medieval mystic texts. As she began to speak, I realized to my horror that the subject of her talk was evidence of digital masturbation by medieval midwives. Excited by the implications of this fragile evidence for occasional lesbianism in the Middle Ages, she was unembarrassed by her topic. She was even less embarrassed to admit, when I asked her what she had to say about theology, that she knew very little about the subject. Indeed, many scholars of medieval theological texts no longer know theology at all.

Yet Christians can be too shocked at such horror stories. They can suffer from too much anxiety of influence. My experience in Eastern Europe, where I have seen faith rise once more like a mighty Behemoth from the sea, proves that our survival is assured. "Culture wars" are not between belief and unbelief, but rather between two kinds of faith. At the foundation of this American secular establishment lies a painstakingly mined and laboriously polished doctrine. It is a faith in the scientific method. Perhaps this is a faith that there can be in fact no faith, but it is a faith nonetheless. "Methodological secularization" is a process that Christian intellectuals wrought and then applied to religion itself. The American academy embedded its developing orthodoxy within an assertion of "academic freedom," a relatively recent formulation peculiarly devised to challenge traditional faith, but reluctant or resistant to affirming it.

Ironically, the institutions protected by academic freedom are the most frequent oppressors of academic Christians. "Academic freedom" is most zealous in empowering both the artists and the interpreters who are hostile to our faith. All over America, chapels have been deconstructed and Christian art, good and bad, has been covered up or taken down. However, the apostles of academic freedom enthusiastically endorse religious imagery if it critiques rather than affirms, "deconstructs" rather than "constructs." Andres Serrano's "piss Christ," with its crucifix immersed in urine, is a clichéd example of what has become a paradigm. On campuses that remove Christ from the chapel, Mary Beth Edelson's "Last Supper," which replaces Christ with Georgia O'Keefe and St. James with the sculptor Louise Nevelson, is a frequently displayed icon of the Women's Center. People off campus, who (unfortunately) but rarely endow or patronize a Christian artist, express outrage over such "extremism." Yet any kid on campus knows that this is no extremism. It is a paradigm. Nor is Jesse Helms, with his crusade against the NEA, focused on the problem. Private foundations and campuses, more lavish than Pope Urban or any Venetian Doge, patronize the undoing of the Christian imagination.

If there is a wonder, it is that mainstream Christians are so very tractable about all this. Like the docile, gentle Christs that their dining room art celebrated in the last generation, they "go gentle into that good night." They feel so secure as to be utterly impervious to what is happening to their children. Trust me as an Orthodox — it takes an outsider to see the mainstream clearly. Outsiders from the Christian mainstream tend to be the ones who expose the hypocrisy in the dogma of academic or cultural freedom. When Marsden revisits William Buckley at Yale in the 1950s, at that time a relatively congenial place for Christian scholars, Marsden sees a young Catholic intellectual who discomfits the still Protestant academic establishment in New Haven because he exposes, in essence, its *own* now secularized faith. And that faith was not, as the academy supposed, objectively tolerant toward but rather hostile to Christianity:

What a believing Catholic could see clearly, but the Protestant elite were loath to admit, was that the Protestant establishment *was* an establishment. By weakening the distinction between church and nation it had claimed the whole nation as its church. Although the doctrines were thus blended with and often subordinated to the liberal ideals of the republic, they were still doctrines. Moreover, they were doctrines with a distinctly *Protestant* heritage.[4]

Buckley, according to Marsden, exposed the Protestant roots of secularism. There is, indeed, a "creed" that has developed within the bosom of the American academy. It is a creed that sealed itself against the incursions of "sectarianism" (by which it now means any theological content whatsoever), but it is nonetheless a creed. But remember, "culture wars" implies a war between two faiths. And this secular faith, no less than our theistic variety, is subject to its own crises of doubt.

Let me return for a moment to Russia, my source of counterpoint and analogue to the American academy. No one would have suspected the collapse of the "Soviet fundament," yet it fell in a historical moment of doubt, an intense and anguished spasm of failed confidence. The Marxist academy of the USSR passed, in effect, like a kidney stone in one of its own inexorable models of "historical progress." Some aspects of American secularism, too, have been systolic and diastolic in nature: the secular generation before the turn of this century was succeeded by a time of revival in belief within the academy. Similarly, it would have been difficult even at Buckley's Yale to imagine the severity, the suffocating totality of the current reign of Established Unbelief. Monolithic though it may seem, the Established Unbelief in the American academy may be far more vulnerable than we currently imagine. Doubt, after all, can be a crisis also to those who do *not* believe.

Faith has its stories of conversion. Agnostics and unbelievers, too, are "converted," and the stories of such conversion underlie many a lunch in the faculty dining room. The common scenario has the bold young academic, most often in the eighth grade, suddenly realizing the sham behind organized religion. Realization in the eighth grade assures that the professor will be more skeptically endowed than his students, who are just now, under the professor's influence, coming to the same conclusions about religion — if their parents were so bourgeois as to

4. Marsden, *Soul of the American University*, p. 404.

convey any at home. It also ensures that for the rest of his natural life, the bold agnostic professor can refute the propositions of an eighth-grade Sunday school class, not the philosophical challenge of a more mature faith. The story, however, like all stories, conveys its truth: the professor rejects faith on behalf of the rest of us intellectuals — students, professionals, artists.

This common act of presumption, sanctioned for every academic or artist who rejects a dimly internalized faith, rests upon a peculiar faith of its own. Carl Becker, the acerbic historian who anticipated post-modern "deconstruction," began life as a Methodist in Iowa. Continuing to attend the university church as he progressively abandoned traditional Christianity, the bitterness of his later rhetoric betrays, no doubt, a vain struggle to hang on to some semblance of belief. "If Methodism is slowly dying in Iowa," the middle-aged Becker wrote home to a friend, "there is still hope for the world."[5] There is a similar sting to his ideology: he ultimately discounted the very possibility of any truth other than inter-pretation (and a melancholy interpretation it was at that).

This exile in a self-reflecting world of interpretation and theory, like getting lost in a hall of distorting mirrors, can be a frightening, melan-choly process. It explains, I think, the horror and despair of so much contemporary art. So much of the creative process depends upon tradi-tion and convention. The acts and values of the artist reflect or strain against those conventions that he or she has internalized. To enshrine relativism is to unseat tradition, dethrone convention. Without borders, there will be no war — but also no real identity. Without meter and rhyme, the sonnet itself evaporates. Relativism begets that crisis in the secular intellect.

In that crisis, however, rests our hope. When a faith, where there *is* no faith, in so evanescent a thing as "interpretation" is what one claims as a dogma impervious enough to exclude those who assert otherwise, the grounds of one's being are vulnerable indeed. Thus the most vener-able of materialist scholars confess to some night sweats of their own. What were those "doubts" that plagued Benjamin or Russell? How unfortunate it is to dwell in a world where hope itself becomes a threat to one's identity.

Outsiders, then, like the Catholic Buckley or Mortimer Adler the Jew, or in some modest way even we Orthodox Christians, can provide

5. Marsden, *Soul of the American University*, p. 372.

a critique of this self-annihilating Protestant intellectual impulse that has bound up the academy and, incredibly, purged culture of its mystic or religious content. Fortunately based at Notre Dame, Marsden's careful scholarship provides the believing intellectual with an invaluable catalogue of the process leading to our present pass. As a "former insider," Marsden does not provide any real solution, but he does suggest one in that cautious manner so redolent of the very thinkers he critiques. It may be a controversial suggestion, but there is a solution. Trust your artists. Among you are painters, writers, poets, and sculptors whom you ignore. Yet they surrender to a Christian imagination, and they can help you to do so once more. They can give you courage and confidence.

And believers do indeed face a crisis in confidence. Evangelicals, marginalized from intellectual life, bemoan their own unsurprising suspicion of the American intellect. Ironically, liberal Catholics have used Vatican II to justify capitulation to an isolating ideology that continues to exclude them *as* Catholics. Never even contemplating becoming Protestant in order to gain acceptance into the anti-Catholic Protestant academy of the last century, they have often shown a ready willingness to secularize themselves and their institutions as the price of entering the still anti-Catholic secular academy that the Protestants wrought. Secularization, the precondition for Jews to enter the academy, was often an insufficient credential. Not until Protestantism had deconstructed itself in the academy were Jews fully admitted, only to be marginalized once more (at least in their male-engendered incarnation) as a potentially "oversubscribed" ethnicity in a pluralist carnival. We Eastern Orthodox, the outsiders at America's religious feast, hardly bear mentioning.

But we have all become outsiders. To be an outsider is now the price of belief. The first phase in the culture wars should not be to reclaim the nation but to reclaim the faith that makes us whole. I am newly sympathetic to "the Christian right," and I see a good deal of hypocrisy in the panic of my academic colleagues as they face this new opposition. The church, after all, has been paying its own way in America. Some of us dare to ask, why shouldn't we disestablish secularism as well? The idea that academics should no longer rely on automatic public funding fills secularists with trepidation.

The Christian right, however, does place too great a faith in nationalism. There is a trend among evangelicals, for example, to reclaim even the most troublesome of the founders, like Jefferson, as a friend. Reading the sources should give them pause. Jefferson as a religious thinker belongs to the other party. (Like Jefferson as a slave-holder, the other party is welcome to him.) I once read, with my class in early American literature, Jefferson's distillation of the New Testament into the more benevolent of Christ's moral teachings. "Distillations" of Scripture — purged of its "naughty bits" — continue to be popular in the American academy. Bled of the miraculous and all righteous moral indignation, Jefferson's Jesus sounded like a rather treacly sort of Marcus Aurelius. It was precisely this kind of Jesus that Jefferson had in mind for the public "nonsectarian" university, of which he was a great advocate. We're treated to another such "secular Christ" in the work of the so-called "Jesus Seminar": a Christ purged of the politically incorrect "naughty bits" that escape simple believers.

Jefferson served up religion's most civic conformity and placed it at the service of the state. In a contemporary context, when the academy has purged itself of all religious or transcendental content, the eye of the outsider can see a chilling continuity. Established Unbelief, if it serves some self-projected model of "justice," retains the authority of the church and Scripture in the energy of its promotion. At the same time, however, the outsider offers the corrective critique provided by a God who sits in judgment over even the king. The Russian czars were shadowed by "holy fools" who made fun of their pretensions. The modern intellectual elite also need "holy fools" to provide them with an obligatory sense of humor.

If, in place of the king, we place the phenomenon of "interpretation," and in place of God's authority we place the state, or "scientific objectivity," or the "rights of the oppressed," we retain the same structure, but not to the same effect. The claims of the contemporary academy are absolute in their relativism, admitting of no authority great enough to provide real correction. "Put not your trust in princes, in sons of men," says the non-inclusively translated psalm, "for in them is no salvation" (Ps. 146:3). Yet if "men" is corrected inclusively to embrace the oppressed in gender, race, or class, the contemporary academy can read the psalm as its own inversion: the oppressed must seize the tools of interpretation and hence seize also absolute trust. This must give pause to any believer. We Orthodox Christians in particular, who were martyrs but yesterday, have recently seen "converted" Serbs, turned from Marxism to Orthodoxy, reduce the great libraries and monuments of Sarajevo to dust in our name, in the name of "past oppression." We know what the moral primacy of the state can do.

Jonathan Edwards in the Great Awakening proved a prescient predictor of what American materialism could bring in the way of intellectual tyranny. But it was the anti-Catholic Whig Protestants who first turned to Europe for models of a militant "anti-sectarian" religion. Calvin Stowe, Lyman Beecher's son-in-law, traveled to Prussia and popularized in the United States his account of the "moral and elevated" approaches to religion in Prussian education. Prussia appealed to him because it so effectively put religion at the service of the state. Stowe sought not a single religious option but rather a state-focused moral education free of sectarian divisions. "If it can be done in Prussia," he insisted, "it can be done in Ohio."[6]

Indeed, the outsider might today declare that in the "political correctness" of our universities and educational establishment, the Prussian model won. What was done in Prussia today *is* done in Ohio: an ethos promoted by a militant academic elite, so nonsectarian as to be utterly a-religious in character, is indeed the primary tool for promoting an internally generated model of the "common good." Yet we also see in our midst an omnipresent suspicion, not of academic elites, but certainly of all elites generated by white males. White males are a category rather than a being. I naturally see myself, among you, as a representative of an Eastern tradition unrepresented in the seminaries, sparsely identified throughout the United States, valuable in its perspective as a counterpoint and corrective. To the multiculturalist, however, my cultural incarnation ceases with my gender and the color of my skin. I am a representative not of Byzantium or of Moscow, the Third Rome, not of the Fathers or the Cappadocian tradition. I am a white male. Do you wonder why I might see all this as a Methodist plot?

This suspicion of the oppressor as outsider acts as a counterpoint to the nineteenth-century American desire for "assimilation," especially of those troublesome Catholic hordes. Stowe and the Protestant Whigs dreamt of incorporating and taming the alien and Catholic other. Contemporary multiculturalists, despite their reputed love of variety, have devised their own revised methods of muted assimilation. They use a single ideological antiseptic, removing from all cultures the divisive bacteria of dogmatic faith, in order to allow the many purified cultures to subsist undisturbed within the one purified state.

This dreary purge of faith exists in cultural texts as well. Book covers

6. Marsden, *Soul of the American University*, p. 88.

in college bookstores proclaim Sandra Cisneros *(The House on Mango Street)* as "the most brilliant of today's young women writers." Celebrating a Latino culture in urban America, she presents a world virtually devoid of Catholicism. Many black feminist glimpses into the "culture" of Afro-America give us a world purged of the black preacher. It is a convenient absence, because the ethos of the interpreter-artist can replace the tradition that so shaped the interior culture which the novel portrays. Through these novels, sustained by a publishing and interpreting industry grown fat on your tuition dollars, your children come to know the cultures that the "multicultural" world represents. The problem, of course, is that while the many distinct "communities" become acknowledged and indeed "empowered" *cultures* (albeit "religionless" ones), the one state has been deprived not only of faith but also of culture. The university, losing a theism upon which to focus, also loses a single cultural consensus to impart.

Cultures with faith generate inevitable tension. Contrast between good and evil, after all, is "tense" in nature. The temporary solution to the tension lies in the purge of religious or theological content, for this alone generates a secular "worldview." Such unbelief creates a miracle: multiculturalism without tension. Thus unbelief contains a greater potential for tyranny than belief ever did: only unbelief can ask a culture to shed its soul.

This loss of soul can be seen in contemporary biblical study. The Bible was once received by the academy as the vehicle through which other phenomena were interpreted. Then the Bible became itself the object of "scientific" inquiry within the academy. Then it became just another book, bearing no special authority, among all other books. This is but the penultimate step in our current progress toward Established Unbelief. Once special by virtue of its authority, the Bible now becomes special by virtue of its potential *presumption* to authority among the non-intellectual, believing non-elite. Thus the Bible in earlier academic models was relativized but "included." It is now, in current multicultural trends, excluded and purged as an object of study or a text to be recommended, precisely because in some cultures of belief it *might* be interpreted as authoritative. The Book has become "anti-book," the threat to all other texts. Its contents are acceptable only if historically verifiable, preferably by non-believers. Of all books or thinkers quoted by his colleagues, says Sanford Pinsker, editor of *Academic Questions,* he hears the Bible quoted least at faculty meetings. (Then he looks, somewhat accusingly, at me, the priest/academic who happens to be a colleague who has never been known to quote the Bible at a faculty meeting.) Be sparing in your blame. The very presence of the Bible, even hints of its resonance, call forth either awkward silence or a faint amusement begotten of discomfort.

A tradition is unlike an individual interpreter bearing the Word. Tradition, being itself an interpreter, can make its own peace with science. Catholicism, excoriated for its authoritarianism, yet managed to deal with the phenomenon of evolution and survive unscathed. If the scientific method *replaces* tradition, however, as it replaced biblical authority in the American academy, then the faith tradition will be allowed to exist only in a curious a-cultural vacuum. But the vacuum kills those who are preserved within it. James Leuba in 1916 embraced Jefferson's belief (and Lenin's) that the academy would ultimately extinguish traditional belief. Leuba painstakingly compiled statistics that indicated that professors were less likely than lesser beings to affirm traditional theist dogma (the more prestigious the institution, the less likely the professor to profess traditional belief). His unsurprising thesis indicated that as education and intelligence increase, faith will decrease.[7]

It is only a short leap hence to assume that a community that promotes education and intelligence will, as a means to an end, surpress religion or at least refrain from endorsing it except as a vestigial, "historical" phenomenon. Thus those Protestant clergy who had since the time of Luther donned academic robes rather than liturgical vestments as the sign of their teaching authority begat successors in the same academic robes who doffed all religious faith — indeed, who claimed its utter untenability in an intellectual context — as a means to their educational "ministry." I sat this summer through a series of lectures by Bishop Spong. On Monday, we did away with the Virgin Birth. On Tuesday fell much of the Gospels that did not agree, by amazing coincidence, with a certain political perspective now prevalent in the academy. On Wednesday we dispensed with Judas, on Thursday with the Resurrection. All that survived of the Christian tradition was bishops. Bishops remained — no doubt to the great relief of Bishop Spong. What we have is, at bottom, a paradox: an academic anti-church, whose mission is to act, in the interest of the state and society, as if there can be no real gospel.

7. Marsden, *Soul of the American University*, pp. 292-93.

As outsiders in America, we Orthodox Christians lack experience
and an academic tradition. As believing academics we can still say, with
a Russian Orthodox pastor at the turn of the century, "We do not live
in America, we live under America: America goes on over our heads."
Catholics have more experience, and those who remain Catholic enough
to earn the ire of anti-Catholics have drawn no less hostility from
Established Unbelief than they have from its forebears in the old Whig-
Protestant established academy. Anti-Catholicism, after all, has provided the one consistent theme in the transition from Protestantism to
High Agnosticism. (One dean, in seeking to explain to me why some
feminists treated me with obvious condescension when I wore a clerical
collar, said indulgently: "Perhaps they think you're a Catholic. Some of
them have been very wounded by Catholics, you know.")

Jews, those other and elder children of tradition, have also found in
tradition a tonic against the excesses of the antireligious academy. In
the contemporary academy, Jewish neoconservatives and Jewish scholars
lament a lost trust in an entity known as truth. Secular though they
may be, they maintain a respect for those Christians who believe they
have found truth in an intellectually resonant faith.

It is time for Christians to live up to their once deserved reputation.
It is time for a new confidence, a new certitude, more than a militancy.
Like academics in the old Soviet academy, however, most of whom
themselves well knew that the game was fixed, American secular academics find it hard to admit that faith can animate the intellect, that
faith is an entity worth knowing. That admission would betray the rules
of their world. Better to let empires like Iran and the Soviet Union fall,
better to remain utterly removed from the imaginative and aesthetic
worlds in which millions are animated every day, every hour, better to
let flames lick at ruins in places that once ignited the world into war
than to give up the rules of the game. There is too much at stake —
position, reputation, career — to admit that the human consciousness
can be affected, indeed utterly changed, by a faith tradition and constant
dialogue, real or imagined, with a voice one accepts as God's.

The answer lies, not in an appeal to the academy, but rather in that
inevitable crisis of faith which will surely arise within it. Liberal Protestants, one is tempted to conclude, made this mess by themselves. It
is a mess with a considerable stake for the moment, but it is one that
the perpetrators and their heirs may have to clean up themselves, like
still privileged but discredited communist *apparatchiki*, as they divide

the spoils. The victory, ironically, falls to the one with the greatest confidence. As a believer I am often told with great solemnity that the state has separated itself utterly from my ways of thought, and that therefore I must be expected, with all my ilk, to foot the bill for myself and all my dreams. Never mind, it will be good for me, says the academy. I am amused now to hear the academy's utter crisis of confidence when those who fund the state suggest that they have now sundered their sympathies from the academy. Is it my imagination, or is my confidence as a believer greater than theirs, as they contemplate the great weaning to come?

Their crisis of faith is inevitable, because that in which they place their faith is now so irretrievably, irredeemably ugly. The metaphors, the images to which they have recourse, like those of Dostoyevski's *Possessed,* repel even as they amuse. Mystics, in their lectures, are digitally masturbated by midwives. This, we learn, was a triumph over homophobia. A famed poet philosopher addressed our assembled students at an endowed lecture. I learned that his art, far from anything noble, was like nothing so much as an infant playing with his feces, his creativity like unto sculpting (forgive the scatology) with shit. Joseph Wood Krutch, in 1929, saw the human being as the most miserable being of all "because he is the only one in whom the instinct of life falters long enough to enable it to ask the question 'Why?'"[8] To join this happy company, the believer is expected to resign belief in order to understand solemn reviews of Gregorian Chant in the *New Republic* that declare that the form has been forever sundered from its context in hopeful, mystic longing.

Call us crazy, but my own Eastern Orthodox tradition is beguiled by beauty. Dostoyevski found it in unlikely places beset by misery, a beauty that saves the world. In place of digital masturbation, sculpted feces, and hopelessness of interpretation, give me a point of reference anchored in (dare we say it) God. In this atmosphere Christian academics should abandon their tone of patient accommodation. There is a point at which patience gives way to cowardice. As Jesus asserts in one of his less pleasant moments, "Whoever will not receive you nor hear you, when you depart from that place, shake off the dust under your feet as a testimony against them. Assuredly, I say to you, it will be more tolerable for Sodom and Gomorrah in the day of judgment

8. Marsden, *Soul of the American University*, p. 371.

than for that city" (Matt. 10:14-15). Our task is to give testimony with a good conscience. The rest, for good or for ill, will take care of itself on that day in which a large percentage of the very intelligent professoriate does not believe.

Yet Christian intellectuals cannot be smug. What have we, after all, *done* for our artists and writers? Exiled them to the kitsch of the American Christian bookstore. Not much of what we buy there is art. We shouldn't condescend to the intellect of the American Christian. If we want those who have been trained in the universities, minister to them. But minister to them *through* culture. Endow our artists — not felt banners, but artists. Give symposia on our novelists. Give them honor, and gild them with respect.

Our source of confidence lies in our midst. Our artists have been ignored among us: musicians, painters, sculptors are the "church mice" of our day, expected to offer their services for free if at all. Yet they dwell in the world in the image, and we can see all around us what a powerful space it is. The artist, and not the television evangelist, is crucial to the process of our reentering our culture. The attacks of the academy, and to some extent those of the courts, are all but complete. The twentieth century has confined us to an intellectual reservation. But they can never stop us from the act of interpretation, of reflection, of "imaging forth" that gospel in which we believe.

Find your artists, then, and empower them. We have made our churches into businesses, into public relations firms, into social service centers — into everything but what they are, reservoirs of the Spirit in a Spirit-hungry world. It's as though we have insufficient faith for the real work of the church. The Christian artist renders holy the process of "image making." We tend to define "holiness" vaguely, as a kind of sentimental atmosphere smelling of the Godly. But theologically speaking, holiness is precise, as sharp as those blades of grass in heaven that C. S. Lewis claims can cut the feet of those unprepared to stroll there. The icon, for example, is not only a portrait of one who is holy; it calls *us* forth to holiness as well. We are all "icons in process," slowly, lovingly shaped by the struggle in our lives toward goodness. That struggle will make us into the image of that glorious saint God wishes us to be. If we surrender our art and imagery to the secular world, we surrender it all. We give up everything.

In a concluding reflection let me return once more to Eastern Europe, where from 1989 to 1991 I spent much time with a dear friend who lovingly restored the reconstructed cathedrals of St. Petersburg. My fingers sifted, chip by chip, through the ruined mosaics of the church Spas na Krovi. I shuffled through the inexpressibly delicate tissue of gold leaf before it was applied, like flaking skin, to the restored rococo flourishes of an icon screen. I heard choral voices rise up to brilliant sunlit domes once crudely emblazoned with aphorisms by Marx. And as a priest I stood and prayed memorials in squares where cathedrals, dynamited into oblivion, had once stood.

What an anguish it was when I returned stateside to find Nevin Chapel, at my home campus, "under reconstruction." The altar was now fitted with wheels, to skid behind a screen where it would be piled in off-hours with the instruments of the band to whom this space now really belonged. The stained-glass image of the adolescent Jesus, resplendent in yellows and ambers, was being concealed behind great folding doors like those of an Olympian cuckoo clock. He can emerge coyly at weddings and such, but only when secular sensibilities allow it. And there was Ron from Buildings and Grounds, precarious on scaffolding, airhammering to bits the large limed cross embedded in plaster above the apse. Its shelled baroque flourishes descended in an empty white cascade of dust. How Soviet, I thought. Those wreckers in Russia who had made a living deconstructing chapels would have been amused.

Professor Nevin, the academic Protestant cleric after whom the chapel was named, was assuredly a figure in the great process of descent that Marsden documents. An evangelical thinker of the Mercersburg school, he dreamt of a rebirth of the grand Christian liturgical tradition, a dream that the chapel had been built to commemorate. I read, once, a volume of his lectures on aesthetics, which rests undisturbed in our college archives. Like Jonathan Edwards, Nevin believed in the divine energy by which the phenomenon of beauty unfolded itself in the human spirit. In his own Protestant way, he could accept the Dostoyevskian premise that beauty saves the world. Nevin, I think, would not have been amused to see the chapel turned into a kind of upholstered monochrome auditorium, however much improved in acoustics. He, I am sure, would have wept.

But Nevin wasn't used to such blatant cultural repression. We Orthodox Christians are. We have undergone, in Eastern Europe, one of the great martyrdoms of the church's history. Here in America, sometimes in the seminaries themselves, an even more dangerous martyrdom succeeds it — more dangerous because it cloaks itself in social righteousness. Those of us who represent that traditional faith for which others have died are succumbing to what can only be called cowardice. There is an assumption around us that the lesser the zeal for theology, the greater the commitment to social justice. The claim is nonsense, but many of us dodge many an issue in the attempt to avoid even the hint of theological zeal.

In the process, we are surrendering culture to the enemy. We give up the arts to those who would imagine the world in our place. Let us resolve to end our accommodation, as artists and interpreters, to this great devolution. We will not lie down to die: in the Orthodox world, our customary stance in prayer is to stand, as resurrected in an unresurrected world. No more submission. No more accommodation. Let us *imagine*, together, what our Christian culture is, in its process of coming to be, among us. Find your artists. Empower them. Support them. Pay them for their work, as you now pay consultants and advisors. They will come to us in droves, and they will make us richer and more triumphant than we could have imagined.

The Calling of the Church in Economic Life

ROBERT BENNE

The economic world in which we live is so vast, dominant, and dynamic that inquiring about the church's role in it is similar to asking each of us individuals what part we have to play in the United States. What role does a single flea play on an elephant? The different scales involved make the topic a bit awesome. But overwhelming size and complexity do not excuse us as individuals from exercising personal responsibility in our own country, no matter how large and bewildering that country might be. Neither is the church exonerated from its calling in economic life simply because economic life is so massive and complex. For the church, as for the individual Christian, the whole of economic life is merely a part of the creation of God, and insofar as we are responsible *to* God, who is the continuing Sustainer and Judge of the world, we are also responsible in some measure *for* the unfolding economic life of the world.

In the following pages I want to sketch what I think to be the nature of the economic world in which we live, the calling of the church in a general sense, and, finally, the specific responsibilities of the church in economic life.

The Economic Context

Though distinctly an amateur in understanding economic matters, I nevertheless accept the obligation to put before you an interpretation of the economic reality in which we live. How we interpret economic reality will in some measure shape our response. So the following represents my understanding of the postindustrial economy in which we live and which is spreading across the world.

There are, of course, many things to rejoice about as we look at the emerging economic world. The world is sustaining more people at higher standards of living. There are obviously painful exceptions to this general observation, but they do not obviate the reality of economic progress. The huge productive engines of market economies around the world have lifted the standards of living of many millions of people. Asia provides the most dramatic instances of such progress, but Latin America and Eastern Europe also seem poised for dramatic growth, as does India. Africa continues to provide an especially sad exception to the rule of economic growth.

Along with the growth of middle classes that accompanies economic expansion comes increasing pressure for democracy. The proliferation of democracies constitutes another bright spot aided and abetted by economic success. Even China, which has installed an enormously dynamic capitalism under an authoritarian regime, will experience long-term pressures to liberalize its political life. In Russia another scenario obtains; the Russians must develop their economy quickly enough to stave off the anti-democratic impulses that accompany economic chaos.

Market economies combined with democratic polities have combined to form a remarkable tool for human liberation from abject poverty and oppression. We must be thankful for the many countries in the world that have employed this tool for the benefit of their peoples. All things considered, the last decades of the twentieth century have been a considerable success story for most of the world as far as economic progress is concerned.

These "successes" have been accompanied by serious challenges that render our picture of the world quite a bit more ambiguous. The integration of the world economy has exerted enormous pressures on national and local economies. Instantaneous communication and rapid transportation made possible by technological innovation have made the world a gigantic competitive market. Most business decisions now have to be made with an eye to this emerging world market. Enterprises must be competitive in this larger context or die. Entire countries who have little to offer to the world economy are in dire straits.[1]

---

1. See, for example, Michael Porter, *The Competitive Advantage of Nations* (New York: Free Press, 1990).

Competition has meant that a good deal of manufacturing has moved from the high-wage countries to the low-wage, or it has meant that simple jobs have been mechanized. Even when firms don't move to low-wage countries there is a powerful pressure to lower their wages so that they can remain competitive. The upshot of this has meant stagnation since the mid-seventies in the living standards of the American middle and lower-middle classes. Some analysts even write somewhat hysterically about the disappearance of the middle class. Though such a judgment is overwrought, it is more accurate to talk of a dividing middle class, the upper end joining the "knowledge classes" who are prospering mightily in the postindustrial world, and the lower end being pressed into the working class, which increasingly gravitates toward lower-paid service jobs. The lower class has more difficulty avoiding the "underclass" as good paying jobs demanding little education become more scarce.[2]

Besides this increased competition, and closely related to it, another feature of our modern postindustrial society seems to be a disillusionment with the welfare state. Economic producers, both corporate and individual, have become heavily burdened with taxation to support the welfare state. In a competitive world economy with stagnant middle-class living standards, a likely target to reduce costs is the redistributive apparatus of the welfare state. Efforts to diminish the welfare state are strong in the United States as well as elsewhere in the developed countries. In this situation the fate of the poor is increasingly precarious.

A closely related feature of our world after the collapse of communism is the waning of the socialist ideal. Only Cuba and North Korea are holding onto the Marxist-Leninist version of socialism. Even democratic socialism, a favorite of religious intellectuals, is speechless before the emerging new world. Little creative initiatives come from this quarter. Even the venerable labor and socialist parties of Europe are competing with conservatives to demonstrate who can tend capitalism the best and preserve the necessary safety net of a trimmed-down welfare state. For the near future, it seems, utopian and even moderate socialist schemes have lost their currency.

The pace of technological change has affected social life dramatically.

---

2. An excellent comprehensive view of the emerging world economy can be found in Robert Reich, *The Work of Nations: Preparing Ourselves for Twenty-First Century Capitalism* (New York: Knopf, 1991).

Marx was right in this regard; change in the means of production results in change in the relations of production (society). Our health care system is currently undergoing major changes precipitated by technological change, as well as by resistance to inflating prices, which are in part caused by technological change. Great fears abound in the world of education that similar changes are in store for it. This commotion makes jobs less secure and tends to break wholistic practices into smaller, specialized parts. Constant job redefinition is a result. In short, it becomes more difficult to see one's work as a life-long calling. Work itself becomes ephemeral and its meaning diffuse. On the other hand, increasing competition amid technological innovation make entry into the economy easier for those who are adept at creating new enterprises. The technologically adept have a chance to prosper in this open economy.

We could not responsibly catalogue the ambiguous effects of modern economic life without mentioning ecological effects. More people at increasing standards of living has meant more demands on the environment. Many thoughtful people, such as Christopher Lasch, believe we have nearly reached our limits.[3] But others argue that more sophisticated technology will allow more of us to live at a high standard without destructive demands on the environment. At any rate, ecological concerns accompany economic development.

Economy — the efficient production of goods and services exchangeable in the marketplace — affects culture as well as society. Capitalism is revolutionary, as Marx pointed out. The massive effects of dynamic capitalism on the meanings and values of the life of the people is only now beginning to be recognized by ordinary people. We are beginning to get populist resistance to the cultural changes wrought by capitalism.[4]

It is now widely recognized that capitalism produces some values that contradict its need for disciplined work.[5] Goods and services are

3. Christopher Lasch, *The True and Only Heaven: Progress and Its Critics* (New York: Norton, 1991), pp. 22ff.

4. A fascinating book tracing populist criticism of capitalist "progress" is Christopher Lasch's *The True and Only Heaven*. Interestingly enough, Lasch, who became more religiously committed before his death in 1993, found the most resistance to the incessant, restless search for a higher standard of living in the classical Republican ideal of political life and in the Protestant notion of calling.

5. Daniel Bell's celebrated work *The Cultural Contradictions of Capitalism* (New York: Basic Books, 1976) argued this point persuasively.

pushed toward the unwary at every turn through the most ingenious advertising one can imagine. The hedonistic value of short-term pleasure is powerfully promulgated. As people get captured by the consumer ethos, their capacity for and interest in hard work wanes. We begin to wonder what has happened to the work ethic; we live in fear that the more disciplined Japanese and Chinese will outperform us in every strenuous task.[6]

Further, we are beginning to recognize that the biggest business of all, popular entertainment, is effectively undermining the traditional moral values that hold together the basic communities of marriage and family life. Driven by the need to sell their products, the entertainment industry constantly appeals to the new, the titillating, the bizarre, the perverse, the forbidden, the immodest, and the shocking. The jaded consumer needs increased stimulation to notice, watch, or listen. In this process the borders of the permissible are steadily pushed back, first in the realm of imagination and later in the realms of attitude and behavior. Certainly it is true that an imagination stimulated by the inducements of modern popular culture does not automatically issue in actions of a similar sort. But it seems very naive to think that there are no connections between imagination and action, particularly among the less sophisticated. I think of the depredations of pop culture as little doses of poison that may not pervert and destroy taken singly over the short run, but taken as a whole over the long run can be very destructive of the souls of our young, as well as the young in other countries who are increasingly the "beneficiaries" of our most important export.

Since any decent and orderly social life depends on restraints on impulse and desire, the breakdown of these restraints in both imagination and behavior become threatening to our common life. Expressive and utilitarian individualism, to use the helpful phrases of Robert Bellah, subvert the capacity to keep the commitments that are essential for the elementary republics of our common life.[7]

A final effect I want to mention with regard to the ambiguous effects of our dynamic economy is the tendency for economic rationality to be

---

6. For an unsettling view of this challenge, see Lester Thurow, *Head to Head: The Coming Economic Battle Among Japan, Europe and America* (New York: Morrow, 1992).

7. Robert Bellah et al., *Habits of the Heart: Individualism and Commitment in American Life* (Berkeley: University of California Press, 1985).

applied to sectors of life where its approach is inappropriate, if not downright destructive. Since an economic way of thinking is so success- ful in shaping economic life, there is a great temptation to think that it will be helpful and benign in other areas of human life. Indeed, the Nobel prize–winning economist Gary Becker has argued that this economic way of thinking is the most illuminating way of understanding marriage and family life.[8] Further, we find economic rationality increas- ingly applied to medicine, education, sports, etc., in ways that erode the practices that are the essence of those respective activities.

Although the foregoing is certainly not an exhaustive picture, this sketch of the economic world in which we live provides a context for us to discuss the calling of the church in economic life.

The Calling of the Church

The primary calling of the church has little directly to do with economic life. At best, its responsibility in and for economic life is one of its many moral concerns, and, truth be known, not preeminent among them. The church has a different, unique calling that is of greater ultimate importance.

That calling is to proclaim the Word of God as law and gospel and to enact that gospel in the proper administration of the sacraments. God has directly called the church to be that earthen vessel through which he reaches out in Word and sacrament to retrieve all his lost and erring creatures. No other institution on earth has that calling, and none will carry it out if the church fails in its essential mission. It is a sacred calling. It deals with ultimate things: the earthly and eternal destinies of all created but fallen human beings.

The church invokes the Holy Spirit to make its proclamation fruitful in gathering a community of believers around Word and sacrament. The church is not a disembodied megaphone; it is the Spirit-gathered Body of Christ. It is a people. As a people it carries a vision, exhibits a discipline, and nurtures virtues through the practices of its living tradition.

As a trinitarian and catholic church, however, it views the world as

8. Gary Becker, *The Economic Approach to Human Behavior* (Chicago: University of Chicago Press, 1976).

the arena of God's continuing, sustaining activity. It cannot turn away from or neglect the world. God's will applies to the whole of reality, not just the church or private life. Likewise, the vision of the church is comprehensive; it has a distinctly public character to it.

Thus the church's calling extends to economic life, just as it does to political, social, and intellectual life. This extension of mission follows from the central core of the church's mission and in no way supplants or precedes it. It is an implication of the mission of the gospel in history. The church's economic involvement proceeds from the flaming center of the core, just as flames spread outward from the point of hottest combustion.

The integrity of the church's essential mission as well as the radicality and universality of the gospel are protected and maintained when the church is guided by a set of themes that provide a framework for its involvement in economic life. These themes are as follows:

- there is a qualitative distinction between the saving action of God and all human effort;
- the church is primarily called to announce that saving action of God;
- God rules in two distinct ways — through the law and the gospel;
- humans are a paradoxical mixture of sacredness and fallenness;
- human history cannot be completed or fulfilled by human effort.

These theological themes provide the necessary clarity, boundaries, and realism for the church's involvement in economic life.[9]

The Calling of the Church in Economic Life

If we are clear about the above considerations, then the next question before us becomes this: *How* does the church exercise its calling in economic life? *How* does the church perform its responsibilities to and for this facet of God's creation? These are practical questions, and in the following paragraphs I hope to provide practical answers. In order

9. I have elaborated these themes in detail in my book *The Paradoxical Vision: A Public Theology for the Twenty-First Century* (Minneapolis: Fortress, 1995). They furnish the underlying structure for my argument in this essay.

to do this I will employ a typology I have used in other places, but here I will apply it to economic life in particular.[10]

The typology breaks into two major parts: indirect and direct connections between the church and economic life. "Indirect" means that the church as an institution does not get involved in economic life; it does not become an economic actor as an institution. Rather, it relies on indirect modes of influence and action through its laity or through independent associations organized by its laity and/or clergy. Neither individual nor associational efforts are under the control or direction of the church itself. In contrast, "direct" means that the church as an institution becomes a public actor. The formal institution itself directly engages the economic sphere. The church's statements and actions vis-à-vis economic life are controlled and directed by its formal authorities.

The following discussion will not include an account of how economic life affects the church and its members, which would be a major inquiry in itself. Interactions of church and economic life are definitely a two-way street. But here the focus is on how the church affects economic life.

Indirect Connections

Before we enter into our study of the indirect connections between the church and economic life, we need to understand several other terms. By "unintentional" I mean that the church has no definite, conscious intent to affect economic life. It has no blueprints for proper economic behavior in the world; in fact, it may not direct its attention to "the world" at all. Rather, it communicates its core religious and moral vision to its members and allows them to draw the implications of that vision for their own lives in the world. Connections are not intentionally drawn between that core and the economic life of society; it leaves that task to its members to carry out on their own.

"Influence" means that the church relies on persuasion, in this case persuasion of its own members. By compelling example, by convincing

10. See, for example, my *Paradoxical Vision*, pp. 181ff., and my "Religion and Politics: Four Possible Connections," in *Discourse and the Two Cultures: Science, Religion and the Humanities*, ed. Kenneth Thompson (Latham, MD: University Press of America, 1988).

narratives, by alluring rituals and practices, by preaching and teaching, and by cogent argument the church persuades its communicants to consent to the core religious and moral vision it bears. "Influence" emphasizes noncoercive means of enlisting people into the church's ethos. "Power," on the other hand, refers to more coercive means to get persons or institutions to behave in certain ways. It includes a variety of strategies ranging from subtle threats to outright force to get persons to do what one wants them to do whether or not they want to do it.

Shaping Heart and Mind: Indirect and Unintentional Influence

The first indirect approach, "shaping heart and mind," concerns the inward formation of heart, mind, and soul according to the core religious and moral vision of the church. It points to the church's efforts to form the inward parts of its communicants — their dispositions, outlook, and habits of heart.

When proceeding effectively along these lines, the church as a narrative-formed community shapes people at a profound level. Their outlook and character are patterned according to the core vision of the tradition. When the church is really the church, its preaching, teaching, worship, and discipline form and transform persons so that their innermost being is powerfully fashioned.

Affecting people in this way is arguably the most fundamental and potentially the most effective way the church affects economic life. Laypeople in their various callings in the world express the core vision that has formed them. Through them the religious tradition spontaneously and often pervasively affects its private and public environment.

Many historical studies have traced this kind of indirect and unintentional influence. One of the most celebrated is Max Weber's *The Protestant Ethic and the Spirit of Capitalism*.[11] In this work Weber argues that Reformed piety of a certain sort, which he calls "inner-worldly asceticism," was crucial to the development of Western capitalism. Those Calvinists were not intentionally shaping a new economic order, nor were their religious institutions coercing that order, but they formed persons in such a way that Protestantism became the harbinger of a new economic order.

11. Max Weber, *The Protestant Ethic and the Spirit of Capitalism* (New York: Scribners, 1958).

How does piety affect contemporary Christians' economic attitudes and behaviors? While there is much material on how religion ought to affect economic life, we have much less information on the empirical relation between religious values and economic behavior. Robert Wuthnow has addressed precisely this topic in a recent book entitled *God and Mammon in America*. This massive study has dramatically increased our empirical knowledge of the subject. In his summary of the book, Wuthnow says, "My argument is that religious commitment still exerts a significant influence on economic behavior in the United States, but that its influence is often mixed, leading more to ambivalence than to informed ethical decisions or to distinct patterns of life."[12] It seems that Wuthnow was hoping to find real Calvinists among his sample but came upon mostly Lutherans!

Wuthnow then goes on to show that Christians *are* vitally affected by their religious commitments in a broad array of personal issues — career choices, job satisfaction, commitment to work, willingness or unwillingness to cut corners, honesty at work, views of money, financial worries, views of materialism and advertising, attitudes toward economic justice and the poor, and charitable giving. People who are more intensely religious are more likely to show distinct effects than are the less religious.

Nevertheless, Wuthnow argues that, while faith nudges our attitudes this way or that, it does so "in ways that are seldom as powerful as religious leaders would like and that do little to challenge the status quo."[13] Wuthnow calls for a more powerful and distinctive formation that would lead to more distinct and disciplined patterns of Christian behavior in those areas.

Thus we come to the major challenges to the indirect and unintentional mode of influence. First, we simply are not forming our people strongly enough into a distinctly Christian vision of life. When weakly formed persons move into secular spheres of life that are dominated by another way of understanding and acting, they adapt too easily to that way of understanding and acting. In fact, the church itself does some powerful adapting and often loses its own soul to secular temptations. And we must emphasize that the economic world has a powerful ethos of its own that is often difficult for the Christian vision to penetrate.

12. Robert Wuthnow, *God and Mammon in America* (New York: Free Press, 1994), p. 5.
13. Wuthnow, *God and Mammon in America*, p. 5.

It is little wonder that economic attitudes and behavior are only "nudged" by Christian commitment.

Added to this difficulty, experienced in every sector of secular life, is the tendency of many laity to view their religious commitments as separate from their worldly economic activities. Sunday and Monday are two different worlds for them.

Nevertheless, the indirect and unintentional type of churchly influence is still an obvious one for the church, as Wuthnow and Lasch have pointed out. Many persons in both church and society would like to stop with this way of relating religion to economic life. This approach seems to fit the traditional doctrine of the church's mission.[14] If the church really does form hearts and minds, people will act differently in other areas of life, including economic life. Further, this approach does not encourage the church to claim competence and spend more energy on issues peripheral to its central mission. It tends to unify Christian communities around their central convictions, not divide them over issues about which Christians of intelligence and goodwill often disagree. Many laypersons, perhaps a majority, believe that if the church really does its job of character formation well, that is all it need do. The church would do its job and then set the laity free to do theirs.[15]

For the reasons listed above, however, as well as for its reluctance to allow the church to address the Word directly as law to the economic world, this indirect and unintentional approach is to my mind insufficient. Without denigrating its importance, we must supplement it with other approaches.

14. Among the family of Lutheran churches, the Lutheran Church Missouri Synod represents this indirect and unintentional mode well. It generally confines its efforts to implanting its core vision into its laity and then allowing them to take it from there.

15. One of the important serendipitous factors of this unintentional mode is the formation of Christian intellectuals who go on to connect their faith and learning in the field of economics. Lutherans have produced a number of distinguished economists who do in fact think seriously about the relevance of their theological convictions to their economic work. Paul Heyne, for example, has not only written a standard text in the field of economics but has also authored at least one book and many articles on the interface between Christian theology and economics. David Beckmann, current president of Bread for the World, is another theologian/economist. Lutherans have also produced a number of intellectuals in theology who have grappled with economic issues. These examples show the power of formation in the churches. There is no way a church could intend that these persons arise within its ranks to become Christian agents in economic life. But it formed them, and they arose.

Awakening the Conscience: Indirect and Intentional Influence

The key difference between the first and this second type of indirect approach has to do with the element of intentionality. In this second type the church does not rely completely on the spontaneous connection between the Christian laity's hearts and minds and the complex and often overpowering economic world. The church certainly does not deny this unintentional connection, but it aims to augment it with more intentional strategies. It strives to bring its religious and moral vision to bear consciously and intentionally on the economic challenges facing it and its laity.

If the unintentional approach could be called the "ethics of character," this second indirect but intentional approach might be called "the ethics of conscience." It intentionally awakens the conscience of the laity by bringing them into a lively dialog between the social teachings of the church and the economic challenges they face in the world.

The Vision Applied. The word *apply* is a bit wooden for my purposes here, for it implies a one-way street. In any genuine encounter between a religious tradition and the economic challenges around it, there is real interaction. The tradition's core vision has been extended by the church into social teachings about economic life. But each step from the core to a social teaching is open to discussion and debate. Some extensions — say, the church's evaluation of capitalism — are much more open to debate than others — for example, the church's teaching concerning the obligation of Christians to be honest in their economic dealings. But all applications of the moral heritage of the church need to be specific if they are to be helpful to the laity in connecting religion and economic life.

We could start these applications with the more personal dimensions of economic life. Instead of constantly focusing on policy matters, about which the laity can generally do little, the church can begin dealing with applications in the personal life of the laity. The issues that Wuthnow has studied are particularly apt: work and its meaning; ethics in the workplace; orientations toward money; materialism; the poor, economic justice, and charitable behavior.[16] One could add other topics to his list: how to choose real goods in the marketplace of entertainment; how to live in an ecologically responsible manner; how to manage one's

---

16. Wuthnow, *God and Mammon in America*, p. xvii.

wealth in one's life and at one's death; how to help empower in a personal way those who struggle economically.

Certainly the Christian heritage has rich teachings to address all these topics. Christian notions of calling, of gratitude, of modesty and humility, of compassion and justice, of covenantal existence, of respect for the natural world, and, above all, of justification by grace and not by economic works are pregnant with meaning for life in the modern economic world.

Fortunately, we now have much material available to us to help the laity apply their heritage to their economic life. William Diehl's many works are particularly noteworthy. His practical efforts to make specific applications are both challenging and helpful.[17] Other recent efforts come to mind. David Krueger has written a useful book that contains much stimulus for lively discussion of these matters.[18] John Schneider's *Godly Materialism: Rethinking Money and Possessions* is a Reformed approach to responsible Christian management of one's resources.[19] One could add many other titles to the list.

The question, however, is whether the church is intentionally making use of these materials to strengthen the Sunday-Monday connection in the lives of the laity. I suspect that it is not. Perhaps if the national and regional judicatories would spend as much time and energy on helping congregations do this sort of intentional connection as they do on issuing statements, we would have more evidence of conscience formation at the parish level. But parishes do not need to wait on the higher levels of church organization to carry out the kind of dialog I am suggesting.

Parishes can begin to stimulate such a discussion by simply providing contexts for laity to talk about their callings in the economic sphere. When this is done, it is pleasantly surprising to find how many laity do in fact connect their Christian commitments with their work in the

17. Diehl has written a number of books in this vein. Excellent examples are *Christianity and Everyday Life* (Philadelphia: Fortress, 1978), *Thank God It's Monday* (Philadelphia: Fortress, 1982), *In Search of Faithfulness* (Philadelphia: Fortress, 1987), and *The Monday Connection* (San Francisco: HarperSanFrancisco, 1991). Each provokes the laity to think seriously about what it means to live as a Christian in one's life as a worker, consumer, and citizen.

18. David Krueger, *Keeping Faith at Work* (Nashville: Abingdon, 1994).

19. John Schneider, *Godly Materialism: Rethinking Money and Possessions* (Downers Grove: InterVarsity Press, 1994).

world. As they articulate those connections publicly, they encourage other Christians to make similar connections.

Other occasions in parish life might focus on more specific issues: stewardship of one's income; ethical challenges at work; tendencies to justify oneself by one's work; the possibilities and problems of retirement; and the economic insecurities felt by so many. The possibilities are endless. Suffice it to say that, without this disciplined reflection on Christian values and economic life, the powerful forces of secular thinking in the economic sphere will dominate and marginalize those very values. The next generation will not have nearly the impact on economic life that Wuthnow sees in this current generation.

Opportunities for similar approaches are obvious at higher levels of the church's life. We need American versions of the Evangelical Academies of Europe, where laity are brought together with theological ethicists to ponder the challenges facing them. Some gatherings can be devoted to particular occupations, others to common issues across the occupations, still others to points of conflict between occupational groups. The church need not "take a stand" at any of these points. Rather, it can act as a "mediating institution," mediating in a grace-full context the competing and conflicting claims of various groups in our society. These efforts could frequently be aimed at the church's elite laity, who are rarely given the opportunity by the church to be challenged by sophisticated theology and ethics in an authentically dialogical manner. There are many high-level Christian owners and managers who are simply not given the benefit of theological/ethical challenge commensurate with their level of sophistication and power in the secular world.

These strategies can also be employed to discuss public policy issues that have direct relevance to economic life. The church, I believe, has spent too much time on encouraging discussion of public policy items about which most people have little say. More attention and effort should be given to the direct vocational challenges that lay Christians experience in the world.

The Spawning Power of the Vision. Before we leave this inquiry into the indirect ways in which the church carries out its calling in economic life, I want to mention briefly another very important indirect effect. This has to do with the propensity of Americans whose conscience has been awakened to join or create independent voluntary organizations to deal with economic concerns. Many Christians join secular organizations devoted to dealing with economic issues or problems. Other Christians begin organizations of their own. One thinks, for example, of Habitat for Humanity, which was organized by Christians and which has been joined by many others who give money and time to its efforts to build low-cost housing. Bread for the World is another such voluntary organization, one that is more directed to affecting public policy on economic issues. Scores of other organizations could be listed.[20]

There is real wisdom in this indirect spawning of voluntary associations. Such associations can deal with controversial issues without directly implicating the church. Further, since they are not under the direct control of the church they have a freedom and flexibility often lacking in church organizations. They also have funding that the church frequently does not have or cannot get.

I have spent so much time on these indirect approaches because I believe they have been neglected by the church. We have neglected the task of forming and persuading our own laity to be serious Christian actors in the economic realm. This is partly because this task has been squeezed out by other priorities in the life of the church, partly because church leaders have not known how to do it adequately, but also in good measure because of an undue emphasis on church involvement in public policy concerns. The churches, especially the mainstream Protestant churches, have increased their institutional involvement in public policy "advocacy" in inverse proportion to their capacity to and interest in persuading their own laity to witness to their Christian convictions in economic life. It seems that the churches become more interested in coercing society through policy as they fail in persuading their own laity to take their message seriously.

Direct Connections

Nevertheless, in spite of what ought to be the church's preference for indirect connections to economic life, there are good theological reasons for direct approaches. The church's calling is not a call only to individuals

20. A recent book has chronicled a number of organizations and their organizers spawned by the church's vision of economic justice. *Loving Neighbors Far and Near: U.S. Lutherans Respond to a Hungry World* (Minneapolis: Augsburg, 1994) tells the encouraging stories of church organizations such as Lutheran World Relief as well as of voluntary associations like Bread for the World. Persons formed deeply in the ethos of the church are inevitably the instigators and leaders of such organizations.

in their private roles; it is also a call to the whole society in a public manner. The church believes that the whole of reality is subservient to God's authority and will, and therefore the church as the Body of Christ has an obligation to articulate the Word of God as law to the structures of society. That task is certainly part of its public witness.

In this direct mode the church as an institution becomes a public actor in economic life. The church attempts to affect economic life through its formal institutional statements and actions. Both statements and actions are direct and intentional. But the first kind of direct connection, articulating social conscience, relies exclusively on persuasion, while the second, exercising power, tends toward more coercive strategies.

Articulating Social Conscience: Direct and Intentional Influence

Typical examples of this approach are the papal encyclicals, the Roman Catholic bishops' pastoral letters, and the myriads of social statements made by the mainstream Protestant churches. Lately these efforts have been joined by the newly awakened evangelical and fundamentalist churches. These statements are not only meant to be tools for teaching the laity of the various traditions; they are also aimed at public centers of power. They are intended to give moral direction to the decisions made in the public sphere.

Pope John Paul II has been an extremely effective practitioner of this approach. He has addressed economic life with vigor and incisiveness. His *Laborem Exercens: On Human Work* (1981) and his more recent *Centesimus Annus* (1991) have both mounted major arguments about the proper nature and direction of economic life. To a lesser degree, the American Catholic Bishops' *Economic Justice for All: Pastoral Letter on Catholic Social Teaching and the U.S. Economy* (1986) was an effective tool to stimulate general public discussion. The Lutheran Church in America's social statement, *Economic Justice* (1980), was a solid piece of work that, like most other Protestant documents, received little public notice.

Catholic articulations of social conscience gather wide response; every director of every editorial page of every daily newspaper seems constrained to comment on the Catholic contributions. But scant attention is paid to Protestant efforts. Why is this? One obvious difference that cannot be remedied quickly is the size of the churches; the Catholic church dwarfs most Protestant communions. Further, the Pope as leader of such a large institution has enormous visibility and carries a moral weight that cannot be duplicated by Protestant leaders. But there is more to it than that. If we look carefully at the qualities of the Catholic statements, perhaps we can identify certain guidelines useful for all to follow.

First, it seems evident that the Catholic statements on economic life draw from their own unique tradition of social teaching. There is a long history of such statements, and the Pope and bishops draw their guiding principles from their own tradition, not from fashionable ideologies of the day. Particularly important in this regard are Catholic notions of the common good and subsidiarity. Such principles give the Catholic statements an integrity and credibility that are too often lacking in Protestant statements, which frequently seem to reflect the secular ideological biases of the church officials who draw them up.

Second, statements issued by the Catholics are relatively few and well prepared. They do not try to address everything. And they devote time, effort, and expense to the process. The Catholic bishops' letter on the American economy, for example, went through three different drafts over at least three years, and the drafts changed perceptibly as feedback from critics was taken seriously. Lay expertise is invited to complement the theological acumen of Catholic theologians and ethicists.

Third, the Catholic pastoral letters distinguish between the central, core religious and moral vision of the church and the important extrapolations from that core. They recognize that as they move from core to social teachings to social policy there is a gradual diminution of churchly authority. Moving through each concentric circle from the core entails moral argument that is open to disagreement among Christians of goodwill and intelligence. For instance, core Christian convictions lead to the conclusion that all persons should get just recompense for their labors, but Christians of goodwill and intelligence disagree over whether the market or the state should determine what is just and who should set that level of recompense. The Catholic letters invite discussion about public policy; Protestant statements too often draw a non-negotiable line between the core and the periphery. Unfortunately, evangelical and fundamentalist churches have recently taken up some of the vices of their mainstream colleagues.

There are, of course, times when statements of sheer protest can become a powerful and necessary witness of the church. When social practice — for instance, the raw economic exploitation of children —

is obviously discordant with the core religious and moral vision of the church, then the church can speak with an unequivocally proscriptive voice. Indeed, it is often much more persuasive to call attention to or protest unjust conditions than to try to prescribe public policy options to alleviate them. The church is a better social conscience than an economic director.

There is another variation on this direct, persuasive address to the society that is perhaps more influential than mere words. That variation entails an embodiment of social conscience in institutional form. In a famous essay on "The Responsibility of the Church for Society," H. Richard Niebuhr argued that the most persuasive way the church could exercise its social responsibility was by incarnating its vision in its own institutional life. He called this activity "social pioneering."[21]

The church has incarnated its own sense of compassion in its many social ministry organizations, which often deal with those who are unable to survive in economic life. The church also models its sense of economic justice when it arranges its own internal life and the life of its institutions in accordance with its own values. In some places it provides means for the poor to enter economic life through training and job placement. It sets up cooperatives in poor lands. It trains farmers and entrepreneurs in other lands. It engages in "responsible investing." These are all examples of "social pioneering." They are done out of the desire to make the church's actions consistent with basic Christian values, but they also have the added effect of awakening the conscience of the secular authorities and giving them models for effective economic practice.

These forms of direct and intentional influence are more controversial than the indirect forms because they put the church's spiritual and moral weight behind certain policies and practices. Therefore, direct influence — excepting the "social pioneering" variation — should be exercised carefully and sparingly. The church simply does not have the authority and expertise to advise the world on complex policy issues. The church should not be left powerless when a really crucial issue comes up because it has depleted its moral capital on a plethora of issues best left to other agencies. It should save its "prophetic power" for the right occasions.

21. H. Richard Niebuhr, "The Responsibility of the Church for Society," in *The Gospel, the Church and the World*, ed. K. S. Latourette (New York: Harper and Brothers, 1946).

Exercising Power: Direct and Intentional Action

The first Sunday I attended a Lutheran church in a changing neighborhood on Chicago's South Side back in the early sixties, the young social activist pastor announced from the chancel that right after church he and other members of the church would be picketing a local dairy company because it had not hired enough blacks. He would wear his clerical collar and carry a sign identifying the local parish. Further, he proposed that all members of the church boycott the dairy's products until it relented. That was direct action at the local level. It entailed the church as an institution becoming an economic actor. It engaged in action — that is, in the coercive activity of picketing and economic boycott. And it did not go over very well among the congregants. Many fumed and left. Others withheld their pledges and argued with the pastor. Most felt that there was something wrong with the church engaging in such a conflict methodology.

The era of the sixties was a time of church involvement in community organizations of all sorts, and, by and large, the result of such involvement was not a happy one. Similar results are accruing around our nineties versions of direct action. Those versions, though of a softer variety than the community organization movement, are expressed in the church's "advocacy" efforts. These attempts are generally directed toward the realm of public policy — that is, they take a political form, though the policies they aim at affecting often have economic effects. Other attempts, however, aim directly at the economic decision making of business enterprises.

These latter usually take the form of "ethical investing." Church funds — stocks, savings, pensions — are used as bargaining chips to get secular economic agencies to conform to the values the church ostensibly holds. Strong arguments can be marshaled in support of such direct action. The church, so the argument goes, is more likely to support causes of justice for the vulnerable than are powerful, self-interested economic organizations. To limit the church's role to individual Christian witness is to refuse to support very worthy causes when we have the chance. The use of the church's economic power is an important tool for serving the neighbor in the modern world. If the church does not use its power intentionally, the secular world will use the church's economic wherewithal for its own purposes. Not to decide is to decide, as the sixties slogan had it.

However, there are also compelling arguments on the other side, which become much more insistent when the church's action is made painfully public. (Usually the "socially responsible" use of the church's funds is done quietly and unobtrusively.) The current fracas about the use of pension funds in the ELCA is a case in point.

In cases like this the problems with direct action become visible. Advocacy gets the church involved with power, contrary to its nature and mission. The church often does "lobby" for its self-interest and therefore engages in hypocrisy when it claims to be advocating for others. Advocacy is usually partisan; it reflects the political and economic disposition of the bureaucratic elite rather than the membership of the church. In doing so it coercively uses the money of the church against the wishes of its members. It extends far beyond what the church has actually said in its social statements, and it has little warrant for much of what it does. It divides the church unnecessarily and usurps the economic vocation of individual Christians.

Do the noble intentions and presumably good effects of advocacy overturn the presumption against direct action? Only partially, it seems. The furor surrounding advocacy is a signal of its borderline legitimacy. The church needs to think clearly and carefully about its involvement in direct action, which *is* fraught with theological, ecclesiological, and practical difficulties. It should engage in direct action rarely. If the church wants to enter the arena of economic decision making in the secular world, it should remember that calling attention to problems rather than "calling the shots" is more appropriate to its mission of persuasion. Further, when the church invests its money it should focus on extremes but leave the great middle ground alone. It should invest money wisely in obviously constructive economic activities and divest or avoid investing in the obviously unwholesome. These limiting principles would inhibit the more activist and coercive uses of the church's funds. It is wiser for the church to leave the more vigorous and controversial agitation to voluntary associations independent of the church.

In some places around the world, however, there are not as many other actors on the scene to witness for justice in the economic world. The church may be the only major independent institution with moral and economic weight. The Catholic church's support of Solidarity is a recent example of such a contingency. Its support of community organizations among the poor in Latin America may be another. At any rate, there are specific, historical occasions when direct action is warranted.

The presumption against direct action is still an important one. Evidence for overturning it should be very strong. As one commentator has put it, "Not to put too fine a point on the matter, religion's capital is frequently maximized when it is not a capital religion."[22]

Conclusion

I have argued that the church does indeed have a calling in economic life. I have contended that more disciplined attention should be given to indirect forms of that calling. I have certainly left room for direct approaches, though without the enthusiasm shown by so many of our mainstream brothers and sisters who have now been joined by their evangelical and fundamentalist compatriots. (I must admit that I do harbor enthusiasm for the Pope's direct address to the world, though I suspect that may be in part because I agree with him on so many items. My Catholic intellectual friends are not so enthused.)

With regard to worldly activities, the church's main calling is to nurture many callings — the callings of the specialized auxiliary organizations to which it is related and the callings of its millions of individual laypersons. These are the primary links the church has with the world, and the church should do much more to strengthen those links than it currently does.

The church's ministry through its laity and its institutions has the capacity to reach the deepest levels of human society — the hearts and minds of its people. Economics and politics are much less able to affect the most profound guidance systems of the people. If religion is indeed the substance of culture, the church is at the very front lines of the battle for society's soul. Its public role as an institutional actor has far less potential than does its indirect role as shepherd of souls. What political party or business wouldn't give its right arm to have over one hundred million people in its lair on a given morning of the week?

Moreover, the indirect mode is most fit for modern economic life, which itself is complex and specialized enough to make it impossible for the church as an institution to speak to or affect it adequately. But

22. N. J. Demerath, "Religious Capital and Capital Religions: Cross-cultural and Non-legal Factors in the Separation of Church and State," in *Daedalus*, Summer 1991, p. 21.

laypersons who are deployed into all areas of our dynamic and variegated economy will be most able to make creative connections between religion and economic life. Further, modern society, with its penchant for autonomy, will be more inclined to listen to articulate Christian laypersons than to the church as an institution. Laypersons will be able to speak and act with the authority of their own economic callings and will be able to translate the Christian vision into economic language and behavior in those callings. All this depends, of course, on the strength of lay formation in the churches. It is to that task that we must give our utmost attention. Much will follow from that.

So we should seek first the Kingdom of God, trusting that much more will be given to us. This priority will lead us to take the economic world seriously, but not too seriously. By pointing to a kingdom of another quality in a dimension of another sort, the church relativizes the pretensions of the world and its powerful economies. It ministers best to the world when it is not of the world.

The Venture of Marriage

GILBERT MEILAENDER

In "this nation of temporary arrangements," as John Updike described our country in one of his short stories, the marriage vow becomes hard to understand. People still regularly make that vow. Often, of course, we may wonder what they think they are doing, and almost as often, I suspect, they may be radically uncertain who or what actually authorizes them to make such a promise. Perhaps they *should* be uncertain in a society marked, as ours is, by easy divorce, by denial that divorce is destructive in the lives of children, by boys who become fathers without ever having had one as a living presence in their lives, by wedding services so focused on the wedding party that the One whose faithfulness the marriage vow imitates is obscured or forgotten. Nevertheless, however baffling it may seem, people still regularly make that vow, and it is one of the few times in their life when they may seek out the church. What wisdom, if any, can we offer the world about marriage?

There is, I suppose, no single answer to that question, but there is a central answer — one that must be spoken, whatever else is said or done. For the church proclaims the God who in his Son "was not Yes and No" but "always Yes," the Son in whom "all the promises of God find their Yes" (2 Cor. 1:19-20). Because we live by the faithfulness of this Son, we in turn must work at learning to be faithful ourselves — learning, as St. Paul says, to "utter the Amen through him, to the glory of God" (2 Cor. 1:20). When we hear from this God a word of command, "You shall not commit adultery," we must struggle to hear in that command his own commitment and promise to us. It will prove true of us as God has promised: We shall not commit adultery. He will make of us people who can say "Amen" to his command.

If the church has anything to say to the world about marriage, therefore, its message must involve at its heart the good of faithfulness. That good I want to explore here. Ultimately I will ask most particularly what wisdom Lutherans may have to offer about marriage, but I do not intend to begin there. We can ask, first, what we know of faithfulness as those who, along with Jews, have inherited as ours the Hebrew Scriptures and the Creator they proclaim. Having done that, we will ask what Lutherans in particular might add to this discussion, and we will ponder the difficulties of upholding the norm of faithfulness within a theology that reckons seriously with sin and deals evangelically with sinners.

I

The crucified and risen Lord, the one who as faithful and true witness is God's "Amen" to us, is the uncreated principle of all creation, the one through whom the Father addresses and orders the creation (Rev. 3:14). The faithfulness that he so paradigmatically embodies will not, therefore, be entirely alien to those created in his image. It is a faithfulness available to all, at least in some measure. In order to understand it properly, however, we cannot begin simply with the language of faithfulness, as if we could deduce an ethic of marriage from the gospel narrowly construed. "Faithful to what?" we must ask — faithful to what intent and structure for human life? And so I begin with what the Augsburg Confession describes simply as "God's order and command" (AC XXVII, 18). If we do not begin there, we will, I predict, find sooner or later that we have nothing definitive to say about marriage, although we may be eloquent in our condemnation of sexual exploitation and our praise of committed relationships.

Marriage is, Luther says in his Large Catechism, "the first of all institutions." The Creator has made us as man and woman, as a sexually differentiated species, in order that we may "be true to each other, be fruitful, beget children, and bring them up to the glory of God." In these few words Luther summarizes two of the purposes of marriage, and if we understand these purposes, we understand why faithfulness is the cardinal good of marriage.

God fashions this "first of all institutions" in order that a man and woman may learn to be true to each other. It is "not good" that the man should be alone — not good that he should have no other to serve, no other from whom he can learn who he is, no other who even by resisting his plans and projects can call him out of himself into a bond of love. Through marriage, that is, God brings us into relation with one who is different from us but who also reflects back to us something of the truth of our own nature. Two people — sharing a common nature, yet as different as their genitalia are different — are drawn out of themselves in order that they may learn something of what it means to serve and love the good of another.

A man and woman brought into this institution do not only learn to be true to each other; by the blessing of God they may also beget and rear children. The God who calls them out of their isolation into a union of mutual love ordains that their union should also turn outward in order that human life may be sustained and friendship increased. Embodying the oneness of husband and wife, the child is the sign of God's continued "yes" to his creation and of his eagerness to use us as covenant partners in sustaining that creation.

To reflect upon these two purposes of marriage is to remind ourselves of the importance of faithfulness. In promising to be true to each other and committing themselves to mutual care, a man and woman have created in each other a set of needs and expectations that cut very deeply into their identity. They have made themselves naked and vulnerable, handed themselves over in trust and confidence. How, then, could faithfulness be anything other than a central good of marriage? To break the vow is not simply to break a promise; it takes on the character of betrayal.

When we reflect upon the procreative purpose of marriage we reach a similar conclusion. We should not need sociological research to make us fear for children who suffer from divorce, although the research is available.[1] For if a child embodies the union of a man and woman who sever that union, the child's sense of self must surely be affected. Parents

---

1. See, for example, the following: Judith S. Wallerstein and Sandra Blakeslee, *Second Chances: Men, Women, and Children a Decade after Divorce* (New York: Ticknor & Fields, 1990); Barbara Defoe Whitehead, "Dan Quayle Was Right," *The Atlantic Monthly* 271 (April 1993); and Daniel Goleman, "75 Years Later, Study Is Still Tracking Geniuses," *The New York Times*, 7 March 1995, B5.

are needed not simply to beget children but also, as Luther put it, "to support and bring them up to the glory of God." And even those who have no such theological context within which to set their understanding of parenthood may come to understand how difficult it is for children who themselves have suffered the divorce of their parents to give their love faithfully and receive the love of a spouse with trust.

If, therefore, the "love of one sex for another is truly a divine ordinance," as the Apology of the Augsburg Confession says it is (Ap XXIII, 7), this ordinance institutionalizes a call to faithful love between husband and wife. Through the bond of marriage God calls us out of our "aloneness" so that we may love and be loved by one who is not just another self; God sustains human life and blesses self-giving love through the gift of children; and God begins to train us in the meaning of fidelity, which we might even think of as the ultimate *telos* of marriage. That God uses marriage to make of us the people he wants was an idea not at all alien to Luther, as Paul Althaus notes: "God even uses the problems which he lays upon married people to help them mortify the old man; and through these problems, they learn the difficult art of patiently subjecting themselves to God's will."[2]

Is such faithfulness really good, or even possible, for us? Indeed, we might be tempted to imagine that it is profoundly *un*natural for creatures who live in time and experience constant change. But that would be to forget our created nature, to overlook what Reinhold Niebuhr rightly termed "the basic paradox of human existence: man's involvement in finiteness *and* his transcendence over it."[3] That is, we are not only finite beings, ridden by time, but we also have, to some degree, the capacity to ride time, to give shape and coherence to our lives — all this by the ordinance of God. The institutionalization of faithfulness within marriage should not, therefore, be understood as unnatural. On the contrary, however opposed it may seem to our inclinations at any given moment, marriage offers not the destruction but the perfection of our love. To make temporality and change alone the law of our being negates an essential element of our created nature: the capacity for

---

2. Paul Althaus, *The Ethics of Martin Luther,* trans. Robert C. Schultz (Philadelphia: Fortress Press, 1972), p. 88. In *Here I Stand* Roland Bainton entitled the chapter discussing Luther's marriage "The School for Character."

3. Reinhold Niebuhr, *The Nature and Destiny of Man,* vol. 1 (New York: Charles Scribner's Sons, 1941), p. 175; italics added.

fidelity within time. To give the last word to temporality and change is to think of the marriage vow only as a way of resisting time.

But the vow is not only that. Rather, it is also and primarily a way "of embracing time (giving love a history by giving it a future)."[4] Rabbi Eugene Borowitz, reflecting the strong Jewish sense of covenant fidelity *within* history, once suggested that we might help ourselves to understand this by considering a choice between two extreme options:

> In one case we will find love, rich and moving, but never great enough to result in marriage. Thus, while such affairs last months or even years, each inevitably ends, and the lovers go their separate ways. The other possibility is of a life spent in a marriage but one not initiated because of love. The couple has very genuine regard for one another, but it cannot be said to rise to that level of empathy and passion we call love. Yet knowing themselves to be unlikely to have a much richer emotional experience or to have a better partner with whom to spend their lives, they marry. Would you prefer a life of love that never comes to marriage over a life of marriage that knows regard but not love? The choice is, of course, odious. . . . Yet, seen from the perspective of time and of a whole life, if there must be a choice, then being married, even only in deep friendship, seems to me far more personally significant than being in love from time to time.[5]

Borowitz sees clearly the human significance — the importance — of fidelity, and the fulfillment it offers us. When the God who is faithful to his promises came to live among us, he came, St. John says, "to his own" (1:11). His faithfulness cannot, therefore, be entirely alien to the capacities of our own nature. As the Son of God did, we can embrace time in our promises and learn to be faithful there. We can give our love a history by giving it a future.

Of course, St. John also writes that when God's Son came to his own, his own people did not receive him. Our attention is directed thereby to the fact of sin, the great destroyer of faithfulness within the covenant of marriage. Surely, therefore, we cannot simply say that our created nature is capable of faithfulness over time. Must we not also

4. Margaret Farley, *Personal Commitments* (New York: HarperCollins, 1986), p. 40.

5. Eugene B. Borowitz, *Choosing a Sex Ethic: A Jewish Inquiry* (New York: Schocken Books, 1969), p. 113.

grant that our *corrupted* nature is often incapable of such faithfulness? I do not want to ignore the destructive effects of sin any more than Moses ignored the hardness of the human heart, and I will eventually make my way toward considering what we should say about divorce. But if we assume immediately that a realistic assessment of the effects of sin encourages us to take more seriously the possibility of divorce, we miss the third purpose served by the institution of marriage — a purpose that loomed very large in the minds of many of the Fathers, and very large indeed in the mind of Luther.

Marriage unites a man and woman in a union of love. That unitive purpose is, by God's grace, ordered also toward a procreative good — the begetting and rearing of children. But now we must add a third purpose: the institution of marriage exists to restrain sin. Modern Christians are always careful to insist that sexual impulses are not evil or sinful in themselves. True enough. Indeed, even in the sixteenth century the Lutheran Confessions could distinguish between the "natural love" of one sex for the other that "is truly a divine ordinance," and the corruption of "sinful lust" (Ap XXIII, 7). We should not ignore, however, what is obvious in human history: that the disordered sexual appetites of sinful human beings are often wayward, that they bring fragility, vulnerability, and chaos into the most intimate of human relationships. We should not apologize for suggesting that when the institution of marriage directs and channels those anarchic impulses toward faithful service of one other person in his or her bodily need, when God restrains sin in that way, human well-being is served. God begins to teach us the meaning of faithful love by offering marriage as a place of healing.

Notice what this suggests. Reckoning soberly with the fact of sinfulness, our first impulse ought not to be to contemplate the possibility — or necessity — of divorce. It may come to that, but we should not think first of that. We should think first that the bond of marriage is the healing gift of God, intended to restrain and cure those sinful impulses by commanding faithfulness. Marriage cannot be such a place of healing unless we permit the vow to discipline and control our desires. Lovers, of course, promise that they will be faithful to each other, discerning however dimly what is truly natural and good for human life. Their affections give rise to a promise of fidelity. But in a deeper sense, it must often be the requirement of fidelity that shapes and governs our affections. That institutional requirement is liberating. It sets us free from the wayward desires of the moment to keep the promise we once made from the very heart of our being. It frees us to be what we are truly meant to be — faithful lovers — even if at the moment that is not what we want to be. The institution of marriage serves not only a unitive and a procreative purpose but also this healing purpose. As such it should be good news for all of us when we are driven by chaotic impulses within, or when we fear to make ourselves vulnerable before the loved one.

II

I have tried to begin where, it seems to me, the Augsburg Confession begins. The Confession does not, of course, treat marriage directly; it takes up the topic only incidentally in order to discuss sacerdotal marriage and monastic vows. But when it does touch on the subject of marriage, it begins not with anything that might be regarded as idiosyncratically Lutheran but with an understanding of God's creation, order, and command — which urge, drive, and direct most of us toward the bond of marriage (cf. AC XXVII, 18-21). We are likely to be misled, I think, if, instead of letting ourselves be drawn back to the biblical witness to marriage as God's ordinance, we try to derive more directly an understanding of marriage from notions of human well-being that float free of that order. A brief illustration of how this can happen may be in order.

In his short and often insightful "contemporary commentary" on the Augsburg Confession, George Forell considered what Article XXIII (on the marriage of priests) might have to teach us more generally about sexual morality.[6] Opposing the Catholic Church's rules governing priestly celibacy, Article XXIII, according to Forell's reading, asks: Are these rules making people better or worse? And if the answer is that they are making people worse, we should change the rules. Forell then applied this approach to questions that were current when he wrote in 1968. He asked, for example, whether a law making it difficult for married couples to divorce results in better marriages — and concluded that it does not. He asked whether laws against homosexuality make people better or worse — and concluded that they make people worse. Article XXIII directs us, he suggested, to a very general approach: "We should ask ourselves what

6. George W. Forell, *The Augsburg Confession: A Contemporary Commentary* (Minneapolis: Augsburg Publishing House, 1968), pp. 92-95.

kind of laws will help people live more human lives. What kind of laws will build a harmonious and just human society?"

More than a quarter century later we may be less certain that it is wise or helpful to seek moral wisdom about marriage while being so fearful of God's order and command. Granting, to be sure, that the law cannot always require everything that moral righteousness demands, we may still wonder whether Forell's is the best lesson to learn from Article XXIII. Having observed the effects of an almost complete relaxation of barriers to divorce, we may be far from certain that it has made for better marriages. And we may well be convinced that it has been terribly destructive in the lives of children. Having persuaded ourselves that sexual preference is a private matter, we find that the conversation has surprisingly moved on — to pressure for *public* affirmation and ecclesiastical blessing. What kind of laws help people live more human lives? That question turns out to be less than obvious to human reason. What looked like a reasonable answer to a serious Lutheran thinker a quarter century ago hardly seems compelling today.

Lutherans need not, however, begin where Forell began. We should start where Christians most often have and where, in fact, the Augsburg Confession begins: with God's creation, order, and command. When we do so, I have suggested, we will see that God uses marriage to accomplish good purposes in our lives — to encourage a man and a woman to serve each other in a union of love, to sustain human life through the gift of children, and to restrain and heal our anarchic sexual impulses. And each of these purposes, in its own way, requires for its realization fidelity to the marriage vow.

There is, though, one truth about marriage to which Lutherans ought to be particularly sensitive, even though it is not a Lutheran insight alone. When the Reformers argued that marriage was (in their terms) a secular rather than ecclesiastical order, they did not, of course, mean that its proper ordering was unrelated to God's creation and command. They meant that marriage was not a sacrament, that it belonged to the order of creation rather than the order of salvation. It was a secular order, but their understanding of it was not secularized, since they "were far removed from the thought of surrendering marriage to the profane, that is, to an order detached from God."[7]

---

7. Holsten Fagerberg, *A New Look at the Lutheran Confessions,* trans. Gene L. Lund (St. Louis: Concordia Publishing House, 1972), p. 291.

If marriage was not to be freed from the moral guidance provided by Scripture, how was it altered when understood as a secular order? It was no longer subordinated to the monastic life, and it was understood clearly as a religious calling, a place in which one could hear and answer the call of God. In the attack on monastic vows — important at the time, though, I think, no longer a concern in our time and place — marriage was freed to be as heroic a venture as the monastic life had been. Thus, Steven Ozment writes that the first generation of Protestant Reformers "literally transferred the accolades Christian tradition had since antiquity heaped on the religious in monasteries and nunneries to marriage and the home."[8]

That this need not be any private insight of Lutherans is clear from the recently published *Catechism of the Catholic Church*, which says in paragraph 1620:

> Both the sacrament of Matrimony and virginity for the Kingdom of God come from the Lord himself. It is he who gives them meaning and grants them the grace which is indispensable for living them out in conformity with his will. Esteem of virginity for the sake of the kingdom and the Christian understanding of marriage are inseparable, and they reinforce each other.

Each way of life is a venture made in response to God's call. But envisioning marriage as such a venture remains a peculiarly Lutheran heritage, a gift to be offered to the world. In his Large Catechism Luther writes that when "husband and wife live together in love and harmony, cherishing each other wholeheartedly and with perfect fidelity," their example "is one of the chief ways to make chastity attractive and desirable." To take up with audacity the venture of marriage, to ask God to make of us exemplars who keep the marriage vow and regard it as attractive and desirable, is a great service we can offer our society. You will find, I think, that many of our contemporaries who contemplate marriage, even when they take it quite seriously, are inclined to regard the vow as a prediction rather than a commitment. And then,

8. Steven Ozment, *Protestants: The Birth of a Revolution* (New York: Image Books, 1991), p. 153. See also Charles Taylor, *The Sources of the Self* (Cambridge, MA: Harvard University Press, 1989), p. 218: "The repudiation of monasticism was a reaffirmation of lay life as a central focus for the fulfilment of God's purpose. Luther marks their break in his own life by ceasing to be such a monk and by marrying a former nun."

surveying the mess so many of their friends have made of marriage, they wonder how they can possibly predict lifelong fidelity for themselves, and they do not know how to take this vow. At best, they think of the vow as committing them to resist time, rather than to embrace it. We should strive to bear witness to a deeper truth: that God has made us people who, by his grace, can be faithful *through* and *within* time, responding to and seeking to imitate the faithfulness he has shown us in his Son.

This understanding of marriage as a heroic venture is, it seems to me, something that the heirs of the Lutheran Reformation might well take as their special calling in our society. We can repeat what Denis de Rougemont once wrote: "When a young engaged couple are encouraged to calculate the probabilities in favour of their happiness, they are being distracted from the truly moral problem."[9] And that problem is that they are being offered in marriage the opportunity to ride time, to give their love a future. If they suppose that they are being asked only to predict the likelihood that their marriage will endure, they miss the call to covenant fidelity, the honor God does them in permitting them to covenant together and thus shape their future.

That truly is a heroic venture, for the covenant is made not only in the face of a constantly changing world where arrangements always seem temporary but also in the face of death, which flaunts the pretensions of our commitment. If, nonetheless, we are so bold as to undertake this venture — serving our spouse in a bond of faithful love and thereby making chastity more attractive and desirable — we may need more reassurance even than the knowledge that God has created us as persons who are made for and capable of covenant fidelity. We may need also to know that our promise of marital faithfulness is taken up into Christ's promise to his church. Thus Althaus writes that, although for Luther marriage was not a sacrament, it gives "a picture of the intimate love of Christ for the church, and we can fully live in it as it was intended to be lived only through the power of the love of Christ."[10]

9. Denis de Rougemont, *Love in the Western World* (New York: Harper Colophon Books, 1974), p. 304.

10. Althaus, *The Ethics of Martin Luther*, p. 89.

III

"Love is not love," Shakespeare writes, "Which alters when it alteration finds."[11] We know, of course, that this is not obviously true of erotic love, which, for all its power and passion, is notoriously fickle and unstable. The institution of marriage is ordained by God to enable our love to rise to the level of Shakespeare's insight — to enable us to be faithful. And yet, in our weakness we are sometimes truant from this school of virtue, and sometimes we drop out altogether, only perhaps to want to enroll again at a later date. What should we say about divorce?

Without ever treating the subject in detail, the Lutheran Confessions seem both to assume that divorce is wrong (LC I, 67) and to assume that the innocent party to a divorce may remarry (Tractatus, 78). In fact, Steven Ozment has written that the Reformers "endorsed for the first time in Western Christendom genuine divorce and remarriage."[12] We should, I think, be careful about how we use one of the reasons that weighed heavily in the Reformers' endorsement. In their attack on the prohibition of sacerdotal marriage, the early Lutherans were struck, rightly enough, by the power of sexual appetite in human life. In emphasizing the permissibility and, even, necessity of marriage they express doubt whether "perpetual chastity lies within human power and ability" (AC XXVII, 28) — except, of course, for those to whom God has given a special gift of continence (Ap XXVII, 51). Insofar as this is simply a reaffirmation of the teaching that marriage serves God's purpose in restraining sin, it is true and useful. But offered apart from the Reformers' own firm commitment to the continued force of God's command, it invites abuse. It invites me to wonder why I should be chaste if I am not married but do not know myself to have any special divine gift of continence. And I can resist that invitation only if I know — in addition to the anarchic power of sexual appetite — that "it is not marriage that the law forbids, but lust, adultery, and promiscuity" (Ap XXIII, 35). No matter how drawn I may be to these sins on occasion, they are contrary to the command of God and, therefore, not truly in accord with my nature.

This same sense of the power of appetite and "necessity" of marriage played a role in the assumption that the innocent party could remarry.

---

11. Sonnet 116.
12. Ozment, *Protestants*, p. 162.

In part, of course, such a judgment was based upon the exception Jesus himself makes in his teaching on divorce as Matthew 19:9 records it. Yet no such exception is stated in Mark 10:11-12 or Luke 16:18. St. Paul's advice in 1 Corinthians 7 in particular makes clear that within the canonical writings themselves there is already a casuistry at work, attempting to take seriously (as Jesus had) God's ordinance in creation while also reckoning (as Moses had) with the brokenness of sinful human life. Likewise, the Lutheran Reformers' willingness to permit an innocent party to remarry was based not only on Jesus' saying in Matthew but also on more general theological and ethical reflection. The Reformers took seriously the powerful human impulse toward marriage even among those previously married and now divorced — and so they set marriage as a remedy for sin against a blanket prohibition of remarriage.

If the church is to bear witness to the world about the meaning of marriage, it must continue to struggle with this tension today. In our eagerness to be compassionate and evangelical, we cannot abdicate the prophetic task of witnessing to God's creation and ordinance. There will be no point to articulating an ideal or norm for marriage if in our practice we constantly disavow that norm. But at the same time, the rigorism of the prophet should not entirely overpower pastoral responsibility to hold out marriage — even for the divorced — as a place of healing and service.

In our attempt to live out this tension faithfully, we will not, I think, be able to argue convincingly that the adultery of one's spouse constitutes the only permissible ground for divorce and remarriage.[13] Even apart from such betrayal of the covenant, a marriage can die for reasons that are hard to delineate and that result from no one's unilateral decision. If we should not hastily assume that this has happened in any given marriage, we should also not deny that it does sometimes occur. Or again, a divorced person who *was* in fact responsible for his or her divorce may no longer be able to amend or revive that broken marriage years later. Shall we say that the venture of marriage in which God schools us in the meaning of love is forbidden such a person? I

---

13. Nor, in fact, did the Reformers. Ozment (*Protestants*, p. 163) notes that they generally permitted divorce and remarriage on five grounds: (1) adultery, (2) willful abandonment, (3) chronic impotence, (4) life-threatening hostility, and (5) willful deceit (e.g., about one's state prior to marriage).

don't think so. As Oliver O'Donovan has written: "The church has to preach the good news that God provided a fish to swallow the rebellious Jonah, and that the fish spewed him out on dry land, at the right end of the Mediterranean, we may suppose, for a man who was headed for Nineveh. The very task that we have fled can be set before us again."[14]

There was also, however, a certain wisdom — the wisdom of seriousness — in the view that only innocent parties could remarry. Such a view took seriously guilt, the need for repentance and forgiveness, and the church's prophetic responsibility to witness to God's will for husbands and wives. In the time and place we inhabit, we owe the world — which includes, of course, the world within our congregations — such seriousness. If we are genuinely evangelical, we ought not to give ecclesiastical blessing to the remarriage of divorced persons unless there has been repentance and acceptance of responsibility for the breakdown of the earlier marriage, an earnest attempt to restore that marriage where it may be possible, and amends where they are possible. Moreover, unless the marriage service of previously divorced persons includes in some form confession and forgiveness, we have lost one half of the tension with which the Reformers struggled — and we have abdicated our responsibility to the world.

There was a time when the tribunal appointed in the Roman Catholic Church to consider a request for annulment included both a lawyer representing the petitioner *and* a lawyer who was designated as "defender of the bond of marriage."[15] There is something profound in that recognition of the church's dual responsibility — to make available marriage as a place of healing and service for the petitioner, and to bear witness to the creation and command of God. Exactly what structural forms this twofold responsibility ought to take among us it is not my task to say, but until we begin to talk about that question we have not taken seriously the witness and wisdom we have to offer the world about what we used to call the holy estate of matrimony.

14. Oliver O'Donovan, *Marriage and Permanence* (New York: Grove Books, 1978), p. 20.

15. O'Donovan, *Marriage and Permanence*, p. 19.

IV

Perhaps this has seemed too somber. We are, after all, talking about one of the great delights of human life. But that does not make it any less serious, of course. Our culture has largely forgotten that when we give ourselves in the body, we give our*selves* — our very person. And a culture that regards with casualness such giving of the body demonstrates thereby a certain dehumanization. No apology is needed, therefore, if we are serious. I have tried to underscore the vision of marriage we owe to our world. It is a place of service — in which we minister to the needs of our spouse. It is a place of fulfillment and satisfaction — in which the spouse ministers to our need. It is a place of service — in which, by God's blessing, we take up the task of sustaining human life and rearing the generation that will succeed us. It is a place of healing — in which our wayward appetites are disciplined, and we are taught what it means to devote ourselves in love to that one neighbor who is husband or wife. And in, with, and under all of these it is a bold and daring venture — to embrace time and, with God's help, shape our future, to be as faithful to husband or wife as the LORD has been to his people Israel and as Christ has been to his bride, the church.

Not just to articulate this vision but to seek to live it within and for the world is both our duty and our delight. The delight is found precisely within the duty, as Chad Walsh so nicely expresses in one of his sonnets on *eros* and *agape:*

> Hitchhikers are justified by faith through grace.
> They do not work their way but wait their way
> To the heavenly city. And the race
> Is not always to the thumbs at dawn of day.
> Many a thumb, at eventide extended,
> Outdistances the prudent morning thumb.
> This, in strict justice, cannot be defended,
> But drivers deal the law of Kingdom Come.
>
> The camera, my bank account, *Who's Who*
> List no merits to claim you for my bed.
> Faith rendezvoused with grace and I with you,
> And good works followed, just as Luther said.

Here at the table, count them one by one:
Damaris, Madeline, Sarah, Alison.[16]

Not all of us are called by God to this venture, but many are. Here we serve the neighbor given to us, the world is served, and God schools us for eternity. These goods — and these delights — cannot be ours or anyone else's unless our marriages are marked by fidelity. When they are, we can give ourselves gladly and confidently in our bodies, we can give and receive pleasure as God intends, we can marvel as the mystery of a child's person unfolds before us over time — and, together, we can embrace time, finding in our lives a coherence that is divinely fashioned and therefore capable of being offered back to God as our own sacrifice of praise. That is as joyous as life gets — and as serious as can be. Chad Walsh, once again, captured the joyful solemnity of human love touched by the fidelity of God in a poem to his wife:

Look at this moment hard so you will know it
When you meet it again. It has no clear
Artistic corners to mark it off and name it;
Yet it is yours; you must be set to claim it
How many thousand thousand years from here
When God at last will lastingly bestow it.

There is the broken fence I helped you over;
This locust tree — notice the blackened crown,
And the long rift that lightning left — this field
With limestone bones half dressed, revealed
Where little gullies eat the flesh; and down
The hill the milky way of faint white clover.

Look farther down, the chestnut lot is there.
Change is permitted there. The bones of blight
Shall be delivered from the foreign death.
The spirit is another name for breath,
And it shall breathe rough leaves and waves of white
Blossoms to break in spray on the blue air.

16. Chad Walsh, "Twenty-Three Sonnets: Eros and Agape," *Eden Two-Way* (New York: Harper and Brothers, 1954), pp. 48-49.

Between us and the trees of transient black
Mark well the little farmhouse and the smoke
That rises in a slowly widening wreath;
We shall not go to see who lives beneath;
Nor shall the ropeswing from the hovering oak
Take you from me and bring you laughing back.

All these can wait, but now look well and see
Not what I am in dreams or memories,
But as I am, remember me and keep
The memory through any age of sleep
So when you waken with the chestnut trees
You will not stand, a stranger, here with me.[17]

That image — of husband and wife embracing time in order to give their covenant a truly lasting future — is the bold and daring vision we have to offer the world.

17. Chad Walsh, "For Eva My Wife," *The Unknowing Dance* (New York: Abelard-Schuman, 1964), p. 1.

Contributors

ROBERT BENNE, Professor of Religion at Roanoke College, Salem, Virginia

CARL E. BRAATEN, Director, Center for Catholic and Evangelical Theology; Co-editor, *Pro Ecclesia*

ROBERT W. JENSON, Professor of Religion at St. Olaf College, Northfield, Minnesota; Associate Director, Center for Catholic and Evangelical Theology; Co-editor, *Pro Ecclesia*

GILBERT MEILAENDER, Board of Directors Chair in Christian Ethics at Valparaiso University, Valparaiso, Indiana

CHRISTOPHER R. SEITZ, Professor of Old Testament, The Divinity School, Yale University, New Haven, Connecticut

ANTHONY UGOLNIK, Professor of Ethics and Humanities at Franklin and Marshall College, Lancaster, Pennsylvania

GEORGE WEIGEL, President of the Ethics and Public Policy Center, Washington, D.C.

ROBERT L. WILKEN, William R. Kenan Professor of the History of Christianity, University of Virginia, Charlottesville, Virginia